Getting Started

A Path to Success to Teaching English to Middle School Students and Beyond

Getting Started

A Path to Success to Teaching English to Middle School Students and Beyond

Anna J. Small Roseboro

ROWMAN & LITTLEFIELD
Lanham • Boulder • New York • London

Published by Rowman & Littlefield
An imprint of The Rowman & Littlefield Publishing Group, Inc.
4501 Forbes Boulevard, Suite 200, Lanham, Maryland 20706
www.rowman.com

6 Tinworth Street, London SE11 5AL, United Kingdom

British Library Cataloguing-in-Publication Information Available

Library of Congress Cataloging-in-Publication Data

Names: Roseboro, Anna J. Small, 1945- author.
Title: Getting started : a path to success to teaching English to middle
   school students and beyond / Anna J. Small Roseboro.
Description: Lanham : Rowman & Littlefield, [2018] |
   Includes bibliographical references.
Identifiers: LCCN 2018041037 (print) | LCCN 2018047107 (ebook) |
   ISBN 9781475842784 (electronic) | ISBN 9781475842760 (cloth : alk. paper) |
   ISBN 9781475842777 (pbk. : alk. paper)
Subjects: LCSH: English language—Study and teaching (Middle school)
Classification: LCC LB1631 (ebook) | LCC LB1631 .R632 2018 (print) |
   DDC 428.0071/2—dc23
LC record available at https://lccn.loc.gov/2018041037

ISBN: 978-1-4758-4276-0 (cloth : alk. paper)
ISBN: 978-1-4758-4277-7 (pbk. : alk. paper)
ISBN: 978-1-4758-4278-4 (electronic)

♾™ The paper used in this publication meets the minimum requirements of American National Standard for Information Sciences—Permanence of Paper for Printed Library Materials, ANSI/NISO Z39.48–1992.

Printed in the United States of America

Contents

Foreword

Teaching the Ways They Learn

In the poem "The Summer Day," Mary Oliver asks poignantly, "Tell me, what is it you plan to do/with your one wild and precious life?"

While reading *Getting Started: A Path to Success in Teaching English to Middle School Students and Beyond* by Anna J. Small Roseboro, readers realize they are joining a vivid and engaging conversation about their own teaching and personal lives. Our planning becomes more purposeful and within our grasp in response to Oliver's poignant question. Should we have any doubts and maybe even some apprehension or reticence about our teaching decision, we are comforted and then propelled forward by Roseboro in our journey as we learn: "None of us becomes an effective classroom teacher on our own. We need active mentors, professional colleagues, and wise administrators" (vii). Through a reflective voice, relevant examples, and applicable lessons with strategies, Roseboro becomes these three persons for us and on our side. We are not alone. We are flanked by her and accompanied in our teaching journey that beckons and unfolds in varied junctures and seams. Indeed, we must teach and reflect on our teaching and learning of language arts and multimodal literacies in the lives of learners. Our students range from early adolescents attending our local schools to adults pursuing higher education in various institutions.

The challenges, journey, optimism, and wonder Roseboro includes in the book make the narrative accessible, readable, and relatable for beginning educators who will learn with and teach to students of all abilities, ages, backgrounds, colors, and interests. The knowledge and experience presented in the book reflects a higher level of care by beginning teachers and purposeful preparation that students seek from others to grow emotionally and intellectually. We learn about the practice of the original definition of the Latin root, *assidēre*, found in the word *assessment*, which really means "to sit beside."

We must sit beside our students as teachers and learners. Roseboro models this not only for us as readers and educators, but how we can and should do this with our very own young scholars in formation in our classrooms across the country.

Getting Started presents the journey that teaching can become and the caring teacher we can be in our words and actions. We are accompanied by other teaching colleagues who believe in our abilities as we get started to teach and learn and to ultimately understand and grow. Our teaching journey includes our students and their families who care and know so much in our presence and work. In our daily work and commitment, we influence our students' lives much like they change ours. We must notice and maintain our momentum in and out of the classroom as we get started and move forward as teachers in the journey.

The novelist and poet Sandra Cisneros reminds us, "There is no such thing as coincidences." After reading Roseboro's first book, I agree. In fact, Roseboro's new book landed in my lap like Oliver's poem did years ago when I began my teaching career. Moreover, this new book sets the stage for a teaching life that is giving, reflective, sound, and wholesome for educators beginning the journey with their "one wild and precious life." You, like many educators across the country, will continue to lean on *Getting Started* for the encouraging and purposeful ideas we read and the optimism we can communicate to our students. Overall, we must engage our students, their families, and our teaching colleagues to attain and apply multiple literacies in the making of meaning, creating new knowledge, and participating in our democracy.

Arise and soar!

R. Joseph Rodríguez
Kremen School of Education and Human Development
California State University, Fresno

Acknowledgments

I acknowledge with grateful appreciation my husband, William Gerald Roseboro; mentors, Robert Infantino and Kermeen "Punky" Fristrom; Jane Bradford, the new and veteran teachers, who field-tested various assignments and sent in reflections and sample student work; Nabeel Usmani, who illustrated for the poetry chapters; and the cheerleaders Laury Isenberg and Claudia Marschall, and offer this book to early career educators across the profession, to educators transitioning to new teaching assignments, and to all who teach and mentor these teachers.

Introduction

If a child can't learn the way we teach, maybe we should teach the way they learn.[1]

— Ignacio "Nacho" Estrada

Few careers in education are more exciting and rewarding than teaching middle school English/Language Arts. Surely, some of your friends shake their heads and maybe even feel sorry for you when they hear about your work with young adolescents. Unless they have worked with this age group, they will not understand your enthusiasm. You and I get to spend our days helping young adults develop reading, writing, viewing, speaking, listening, and studying skills needed for success wherever their career path takes them. The same is true of students at any age. Our work is challenging but also has lots of fun; we get to share our love of language and literature, speaking, and writing—and cultivate such love in our students. We not only must know, understand, and love language arts content but must also know, understand, and love our learners in all of their remarkable diversity.

TEACHING AND WRITING ABOUT TEACHING

As a candidate for National Board Certification for Early Adolescent/English Language Arts, I reflected seriously about what, how, and why I teach. Others were interested and requested more explanation. From those conversations and feedback from my presentations and workshops, I recognized the importance of sharing valuable practices. So, I began putting my rationales, ideas, and lessons into words.

Novice teachers are thirsting for solidly structured lessons used by successful experienced teachers. I observed this at new teacher receptions held by the California Association of Teachers of English and Michigan Council of Teachers of English. Many begin teaching without the benefit of local mentors. They are enthusiastic but soon face tough standards and accountability; they are unsure of how to serve early adolescent students in an increasingly culturally and linguistically diverse assessment-driven environment.

They want to affirm these diversities with specific long-range goals that align with school curriculum standards to prepare students for college or careers. Few states offer special courses designed for teaching middle school students or new adult students. Emergency credentialing is offered by many states to satisfy the rising demand for new teachers especially in culturally diverse communities. These concerns, among others, compelled me to record and share my experiences teaching students across the country.

GROWING PROFESSIONALLY

None of us becomes an effective classroom teacher on our own. We need active mentors, professional colleagues, and wise administrators. We all must continue growing professionally throughout our years of service. Why? Pedagogies change. So do the cultures our students come from. Standards of and for assessment also change. Furthermore, the technological environments in which our students live are continuously shifting. It is critical that we constantly learn from one another how to tap into these social and technological dynamics. We must admit, too, that differences in our ages, even generations, are factors in adapting successfully. A colleague says that we teach at the constantly changing intersection of old and new.

I have benefited from years of formal study, involvement in professional organizations, conferences and workshops, reading journal articles, online conversations, advice from generous colleagues, and years of teaching students from middle school to graduate college. Consequently, the lessons in the book are informed by philosophies and theories from a variety of sources, as well as four decades of experience as an English/language arts teacher, college instructor, and mentor to early career educators across the nation. Several classroom teachers across the nation have adopted or adapted these lessons successfully and affirm the practices in their reflections.

Publications by the National Middle School Association and the National Research Council have proven invaluable and affirm that middle school curricula must be challenging, integrated, and exploratory. Years ago Howard Gardner proposed the existence of a number of relatively autonomous intelligences: linguistic, logical, musical, spatial, bodily kinesthetic, interpersonal, and intrapersonal. And Django Paris recently published advice about cultural relevance and social justice guiding education instruction practices. These views are reflected in lessons described in this book.

SERVING STUDENTS ARTFULLY

The writings of Louise Rosenblatt and Fran Claggett inspired me to incorporate assignments accommodating many of Gardner's multiple intelligences. Rosenblatt encourages educators to allow students to respond to reading in their own ways—that students should rely on prior knowledge to help them make sense of the literature. You also will find lessons incorporating concepts of reciprocal reading as described by Paliscar and Brown.

These approaches to reading and interpretation of literature free us from the burden of focusing only on what literature means. They give us permission to let literature speak to students and help us trust their responses about what it says to them in their own cultural contexts and developmental stages. Nevertheless, the literature has to be taught, standards must be met, and students must demonstrate academic proficiency. You must plan lessons that require students to ground their responses in the texts, demonstrating their grasp of knowledge, understanding of concepts, and acquisition of skills. Otherwise they can stray too far afield during class discussions or while writing about the literature.

Here are theory-based lessons to help you plan units for the range of students you teach. Specific assignments for the course of a school year take into account myriad ways adolescents can be taught and assessed based on specific ages and maturation, as well as individual learning styles and cultural experiences. I readily admit that such a variety of lessons have been developed this way to maintain my own interest; I thoroughly enjoy learning with and from my students.

Each time you offer your students the option to demonstrate understanding of literature and life, you gain greater insight into fiction and nonfiction works you are studying together. You also form a deeper understanding of students and their ways of looking at text and at the world around them. At the same time, you have confidence that you are on the road to fulfill the charge of preparing students for future success.

LOOKING FOR THE CURRICULUM?

Unless you have taken a college course in or are a devotée of young adult literature, chances are you are not familiar with much of the literature that you are being asked to teach. You may discover that literature in your own middle school curriculum is very different from what you read as a student. My advice? Do not worry about your lack of background. While it is important for you to read all the literature in the curriculum, it is not crucial for you to have studied all the academic texts you are using.

Most middle school curricula require students to learn about different kinds of texts—how to read them, recognize their structure, identify the function—and understand the purpose of literary structure and rhetorical devices and, of course, how to talk and write about those texts intelligently. The schools are often less concerned about the specific titles used than they are about students' ability to read and understand any kind of writing—fiction and nonfiction, in print or digital formats. Therefore, it is important to develop a range of strategies for teaching various texts in a culturally sustainable climate so that you can adapt to the reading lists in schools or districts that employ you.

CHOOSING ALTERNATIVE WAYS TO TEACH AND ASSESS

Reading is not the same as comprehension. Once students have read assigned stories, plays, articles, essays, and poems, you must determine how well the students understand them. Fran Claggett, a pioneer in the use of graphics in teaching literature, recommends that teachers employ art—either via graphics to help plot out the structure before or after the students read, or via assignments for which students can use art to show what they know. Today, the word "graphics" seems anachronistic. So do the terms "visuals" and "media," let alone "audiovisual."

Our twenty-first-century students are more versed in digital, computerized media. Yet the basics of literature as art and story have not changed. Whatever the medium, there still is skillful use of language and imaginative use of arrangement. Therefore, lessons in this book incorporate old and new media to show students a work's traditional devices, such as structure and plot lines, images, and symbols. With proper guidance, students can use their artistic interests and digital talents to demonstrate comprehension of even the most traditional literature, sophisticated essays, and multimodal environments.

What I also like about using art and digital media is the fact that I am neither an artist nor a techy, so my students get to see me at my mediocre best. Students see they can produce something better because drawing is clearly not one of my strengths. They often are more adroit at working with computer applications and digital media creating their own podcasts and making their own movies. More students seem inclined to risk being vulnerable when they see me somewhat unartfully expressing what literature means to me.

Artistic diversity goes beyond linguistic modes of reading, writing, and speaking. You can discover in this book that such diversity can help a wider range of students to shine before their peers, building self-esteem among some of those who need it most. You soon realize that incorporating art and technology enhances your instruction, improves student engagement, and increases learning.

In other words, reduce your students' insecurities and design lessons that build confidence and develop their strengths. Let students use music or dance to express the mood of literary works or characters in those works, and even the tone of an assignment's article or video. Invite your students to act out scenes, partly to assist kinetic learners and partly to give all your energetic adolescents an opportunity to get out of their seats and move around. When auditory and visual learners see the work of their peers, they too are learning at a deeper level.

Language arts learning is more than demonstrating competence in traditional linguistic modes. For that reason, assignments in this book give more students an opportunity to shine individually before their peers by employing the range of their multimedia abilities to specific language arts learning. Several are not nearly as time consuming to grade as a written assignment, yet are equally revealing and authentic.

TEACHING PRESERVICE TEACHERS
AND GRADUATE SCHOOL STUDENTS

When I moved from California to Michigan and became an adjunct education professor at a state university, I noticed that preservice students eagerly latched on to the study of literacy assessment. They impatiently leaned forward to hear about instructional practices useful in guiding developmentally appropriate learning. These students recognized through their internship assignments in local classrooms that being able to provide instruction is only half the responsibility of teachers. The other half is choosing or developing formative assessment tools that demonstrate what students are learning and then designing subsequent lessons based on data revealed in these assessments.

After working a few years in the classroom, graduate students found it beneficial to spend their summer examining research theories, differentiated instruction, and assessment practices appropriate for the literacy needs of their students and crafting curricula to meet those needs. When it comes to assessing, we do our best based on when we are clear about we are trying to measure and what our measurements tell us about our students. Some of the lessons that follow may stretch you and even pull you further along than you thought possible as you strive to reach course standards without teaching solely for the tests. That is fine. We teachers have to be students ourselves, learning by doing and assessing.

UNDERSTANDING WHAT IS APPROPRIATE FOR MIDDLE SCHOOL

Perhaps the notion that most influences effective instruction for middle school students is that they tend to work well in groups. Yet you must design such group lessons to maximize individual student learning. In the early weeks of the semester, you recognize the importance of using more teacher-directed instruction, demonstrating manners, modeling lessons, and giving students opportunities to develop behaviors for successful group activities throughout the year.

For this reason, a rule of thumb is student choice/teacher control. This may be another way of applying Vygotsky's notion of the zone of proximal development or the Pearson and Gallagher idea known to many as the gradual release of responsibility. You are responsible for planning lessons that provide opportunities not only for student learning in different ways from different sources but also for designing lessons that deliberately lead to meeting standards established by your respective schools, districts, and states so your students increasingly become more self-disciplined and independent learners.

One early career educator shared that one of her greatest challenges as a new middle school teacher was appropriately and effectively monitoring her teaching and meanwhile maintaining a positive classroom atmosphere. In a sixth-grade charter school that focused on building character as well as strong academics, she found it difficult to set the right tone at the beginning of the year. Student choice began to swamp teacher control. When it came time for formal assessment, she realized that it would have been better to phase in student choice more gradually during the first semester. She loved the students and students loved learning from her, but she had not tied the pedagogy to assessment as well as she would have liked. That need not be a problem for you.

KNOWING WHAT YOUNG ADOLESCENTS ENJOY

Young adolescents enjoy talking and often learn well from each other. As *Turning Points 2000: Educating Adolescents in the 21st Century* puts it, Reutzel and Cotter affirm that "Cooperative learning . . . can be a successful technique both to teach content and to raise self-esteem among all students particularly those whose native language is not English."[2] Adolescents are very sensitive to perceptions of their peers. Healthy learning environments have both cooperative and project-based learning to enhance relationships among different social and ethnic groups. Therefore, it is good to structure frequent lessons that give students permission to do what they love to do: talk to one another. The key words here are *structure* and *talk.*

Once the students begin working together, regularly circulate among groups, listening in, giving assistance as needed. You begin to discover in an informal but intentional way what ideas they have grasped, what areas need further instruction, and whether the students are ready for more formal assessment demonstrating their readiness to move on to the next level of instruction. As often as appropriate, include assessments where pairs and small groups of students can use the new technologies, even if they are more familiar to your students than to you. By teaching each other how to "do" language arts via newer as well as older media, students teach themselves and often you, the teacher, as well.

While students prepare together for group or student-led discussion, they are also reviewing lessons in more depth than they might have if working solely individually. Students are then participating in the necessary preconditions for quality: content, collaboration, and choice. Collaborating on projects can produce mutual learning.

BALANCING STRUCTURE WITH CHOICES

While offering students lots of choice in reading, writing, and responding is important, the key to becoming an effective teacher is establishing structures and routines on which students can depend. These structures and routines foster important habits: using time efficiently; maintaining useful notebooks and digital files for test and exam preparation; reading and writing efficiently; and participating cooperatively in small-group or full-class discussions, as well as using technology with a critical eye and creative bent.

Good habits help students learn the basics of language and forms of literature, including essays, novels, poetry, and drama. When students know daily class requirements and routines, they have something against which to rebel without rejecting it completely. In a workshop titled "You Are Not Going Crazy, This Really Is Normal Behavior," one presenter declared that once adolescents know the boundaries, they frequently challenge them, but they usually comply.

Experience has shown that even though middle school students love to try the system and test the rules—just to see how teachers respond—they also appreciate predictability. For some students, a dependable pattern gives them a sense of control and power. They know what to expect and how to perform amid their own physical and emotional changes.

For these reasons, lessons early in the school year are designed like benevolent training sessions in an athletic program, providing opportunities for participants to learn the rules of games and to develop knowledge and skills for success. The effective, experienced teachers you observe only seem to handle this training period effortlessly; such veterans know how to offer student choices within a fair but firm classroom structure.

REMOVING THE SCAFFOLDS

As the school year progresses, you can step aside and become more of a coach than an instructor. If all has gone well, students already know the kinds of reading, writing, media, speaking, and listening skills they must learn. You have shown them course standards, which you all are striving to reach. Goals of the course should not be a secret. As with fellow travelers, if everyone knows where you are going, all can be alert and supportive along the road. Even backseat drivers can come in handy.

You can then increase the number of choices for students to practice these skills more independently and demonstrate their growing knowledge and skills even more creatively. As you move on, students soon learn how to act and what to do because they develop habits of mind, as well as confidence and competence to handle tasks presented them. They rise to the challenge of future goals as they see evidence they are meeting earlier ones. Happily, they begin to enjoy the learning. When adolescents feel secure, they are able to function more effectively, bringing joy to all involved.

While I tend toward student choice over teacher control, my goals are always student centered. What is it that students want and need to know and do by the end of the school year? What kind of nurturing, culturally sustaining environment must be developed, and experiences offered, to ensure students reach these goals? For young adolescents with a novice teacher, this may mean a little more visible structure than would be evident in the classroom of a veteran teacher. While I recognize that many approaches to teaching can be effective, the ideas I share are those that have worked well for me and the new-to-mid-career teachers I mentor.

In this book are comments both about my experience teaching young adolescents and about descriptions of specific lessons you can use throughout a full school year. These lessons are structured to get to know the students and introduce the course's main concepts. You can find interdisciplinary lessons that encourage students to use knowledge learned in social studies, science, music, and art. Some lessons are designed to increase students' understanding and ease with library and online research while meeting the language arts standards you are required to address.

ACKNOWLEDGING PHYSICAL AND EMOTIONAL CHALLENGES

The primary challenge in teaching middle school is that physical, emotional, and social issues often overwhelm and distract students. Both male and female students can be manically mischievous one day and dismally depressed the next.

Be prepared by designing lessons that keep them excited about learning to use receptive and expressive language arts. Such skills can help them succeed personally and academically. You could view yourself as a ship's captain whose charge is to chart a course that provides safe passage through the tumultuous preteen and early teen years. As captain, you recognize the need for balancing structure and choice. Though you already know expected standards, as the year goes, you develop a clearer vision of where you are going and how to get there. You learn more specifically what this year's students need to know and do. You also discover that they prefer contributing to the journey. You may even begin envisioning the curriculum as the ship, the units as the decks, and the lessons as the rooms. Within the ship, upon the decks, and inside the rooms, there are choices the students can make.

As you become more acquainted with your traveling companions, you find yourself adopting and adapting strategies that best keep them—and you—engaged, moving progressively from port to port. Eventually more of your students complete the journey ready to step on the firmer, more solid ground of high school territory with self-assurance and proficiency, prepared for challenges awaiting them.

APPLYING NATIONAL WRITING PROJECT CONCEPTS

After becoming a San Diego Area Writing Project fellow, I began incorporating the National Writing Project's sequencing strategy of fluency, form, and correctness and soon noticed that both my students and I were more enthusiastic about learning. Sequencing lessons this way gives students time to write frequently, conduct peer editing, revise, edit, and publish in a variety of ways for a wide range of audiences. With more ready access to technology, it is easier to publish regularly for real audiences. They may be parents logging onto the class website or students in classes overseas who are participating in collaborative reading and flexible assignments that invite students to write for different purposes—to explore, explain, expand, and even entertain.

The lessons described in this book also show ways to reduce the time-consuming burden of grading each piece of writing for correctness. Following the recommendations here, you begin to see the benefits of reading some students' writing or viewing their media projects just to discover whether they comprehend a specific text or just what they think about a particular topic. As a result, you can enjoy the freedom to read or view some assignments only for the ideas presented.

These kinds of writings and media productions become no-stress formative assessments. As you determine what students think, know, understand, and can do, you can adjust your instruction based on what you have observed and read. When students realize that every word they write or image they project may not be evaluated for correctness, your otherwise self-conscious young teens become more fluent. They are willing to write more often, and they also appreciate that you give them some choice about what writing, print, or digital media they wish to submit to peer editing, evaluation, and publishing.

PRESENTING, PRACTICING, AND PROVING

For the veteran educators looking to revive or revise their instruction or the novice looking to rev up for the first year of teaching, here are proven ways to manage grading and assessments and strategies for students to reflect and assess their own work. Throughout the book, note connections to the language arts standards of the National Council of Teachers of English and International Literacy Association, which reflect curriculum standards in most states.

Although specific standards change occasionally, they still address the basic goal of applying traditional literacies in new literacy contexts. At the same time, the Common Core Standards for English language arts charge educators to design lessons that equip students with knowledge and skills for college and career readiness when they complete their first twelve years of schooling. Managing both charges requires time and talent, effort and efficiency.

Some chapters include examples of student-written responses to assignments and comments on what that writing reveals about student learning. They may help expand your insight and prepare you for what to expect as you accept the challenge and come to value teaching English language arts in any courses you teach.

Other ideas are on the companion website for this book http://teachingenglishlanguagearts.com. All are designed to prepare you for presenting engaging lessons designed to give students opportunities for practicing English language arts skills, proving to you and themselves that they are maturing as students under your tutelage.

REACHING THE ULTIMATE GOAL:
TO ENJOY TEACHING

To support you in your early years and sustain you along the road, to enable you to remain an engaged, enthusiastic, and effective teacher of English language arts in the middle school and beyond, here are ideas to develop and present lessons that meet students' emotional and intellectual needs while challenging them to complete increasingly complex tasks. When students are learning and you can document that learning through appropriate assessments, both you and your students enjoy more of your time together. It is my goal to offer you practical and proven practices that bring you the kind of pleasure in teaching and mentoring early career educators that I have experienced for so many years.

NOTES

1. Ignacio "Nacho" Estrada, Think Exist, n.d. http://thinkexist.com/quotes/ignacio_estrada/ (May 31, 2012).
2. Quoted by D. Ray Reutzel and Robert B. Cotter, Jr., "Classroom Reading Assessment." In *Strategies for Reading Assessment and Instruction: Helping Every Child Succeed*, 2nd Ed (New Jersey: Merrill-Prentice Hall, 2003), p. 26.

Chapter 1

Scoping Out the Year in Preview: Plan Now to Be Effective and Efficient

The mediocre teacher tells. The good teacher explains.
The superior teacher demonstrates. The great teacher inspires.[1]

—William A. Ward

Each school year is a journey, somewhat like leading an extended tour with young people you have just met. You want to be ready for the unexpected, learning and adjusting as you go, keeping in mind, you are in charge. In the era of standardization, it still is important to customize the trip and personalize instruction, alert to who you will be teaching, what you are required to teach, and the fact that you are a professional in the classroom. One way of making the trip effective is to understand aspects of it you can control and which you cannot. Even with class lists (or list of passengers) and a curriculum (or an itinerary) you receive, you can incorporate personal touches that reflect the unique qualities you bring to the work based on your own interests and experiences.

It may seem odd, but a good place to begin planning and personalizing instruction for a whole school year is to focus on school holidays, breaks, and vacations. Aha! You recall from your own days as a student that how challenging it was to be attentive the few days before and after any of these three! Among the ways you can assure you stay on course is by considering ways to maximize instruction on potentially lost days.

Take into consideration ethnicities and cultures of students in your classes. What holidays do they share in common? Which are unique to a few? How can you integrate into your lessons the wealth of information, experience, and passion surrounding holidays, breaks, and vacations? Subtler to think about is the emotional and physical drain, say, on your Jewish and Muslim students who, for cultural or religious reasons, may be fasting on a day you planned to

1

Plan with school breaks in mind

schedule a major test. Many Asian families observe their calendar New Year with days of celebrations that may run late into the evening making it difficult for students to attend to homework.

One way to connect with students personally is letting them know that *you* know, without making them the center of censure by peers who may not understand. What about rodeo and sports tryouts, dance recitals, Bar and Bat Mitzvahs, and confirmations? The middle school years are when students are more easily sidetracked by such rites of passage and out-of-school events. Older students have comparable enticements. What kind of reading, writing, active learning, critical thinking, and even reflection can you organize to redeem the time and channel the energy of easily distracted students?

In addition to knowing the cultures and ethnicities of your students, it is important to learn a little more about them, their families, and circumstances in which they live. How much do you know about resources available in the community where your school is located or your students live? Are there local libraries with technology available? Once you have your class lists, take a look at any notices regarding special physical or emotional needs. Plan time to meet with support staff and paraprofessionals with whom you will share students.

What are you learning that may impact the way you set up your classroom or design lessons? In conversations with veteran teachers, what can you learn about the most efficient ways to initiate and maintain communication with families regarding languages spoken at home and their access to technology? What is required at your school? Do you have a choice to contact by phone or e-mail? Just as a tour company would gather this information before the trip begins to help insure the safety and success of its clients, so should a teacher commit to being ready for those inherent eventualities. As in scouting, you want to be prepared.

One of the most respectful things you can do for your students is to learn to pronounce and spell their names. If you happen to be teaching in a community with a very diverse population, consider getting someone to help you with pronunciation or use online sites like www.pronouncenames.com, where you can hear names from many nationalities pronounced. Imagine the pleasant surprise for students who seldom hear their name spoken correctly to hear it from you on the first day of school! Even if you do not say them all perfectly, the fact that you care about each student as a person will gain their respect. The students will see you trying, and they may be willing to do the same.

PERSONALIZING THE CLASSROOM

All right—on to personalizing instruction for the journey! Think about ways you can prepare the following:

- Reflect the personalities/cultures of you and your students
- Display a list of acceptable standards of conduct
- Share guidelines for grading
- Devise ways to tailor lessons for the combination of students who make up the classes each year
- Select efficient ways to measure learning that provide valid information without becoming swamped with minutiae
- Most important, preplan ways to stay healthy until journey's end

KNOW WHERE YOU ARE GOING

Even before preplanning a trip, one must know the destination. As soon as possible, review requirements for the course set forth by your school, district, or state. In what specific ways are you expected to prepare your students for success in college or careers based on the standards for English language arts for your school's curriculum? Know these well enough to state in your own words the portions of the curriculum you will be required to teach in your assigned courses. Then work backward. You will want to include answers to questions such as given here:

- What do students need to know and be able to do at the end of the school year?
- How will I learn what they know and are able to do by the end of our time together?
- What do they know already?
- How can I learn what they know and are able to do already?
- What kind of lessons and experiences can I design to provide opportunities for students to learn with and from one another, and ultimately, to acquire the knowledge and develop the skills they need to have by the end of the school year? In other words, how will I know we have arrived at our destination?
- What resources are available—in my classroom and building or school site—to my students in the classroom, in the building, or at home?
- How can I collaborate with teachers within my department and across the content areas to design lessons linking what students are learning in other classes to what I am required or able to teach? Most people think of social studies and science for collaboration. Consider the arts, physical education, health, and tech classes.
- What will make teaching this course fun and interesting for me?

Once you can answer these questions—in writing—you can begin to select from resources you have on hand and then request or assemble those required to meet your students' needs.

The physical space where you teach can support your instruction. Think about ways you can make your classroom attractive and inviting, knowing that one does not need to be wealthy or artistic to do so. It is possible to begin the school year with a bulletin board covered with an attractive neutral color and labeled "Student Work," a welcome sign, and an inspiring thought for the week; leave the rest blank.

During the first week, have lessons that call for small group or individual art work that you can post on your bulletin boards. You will have the control of designing lessons that show what you would like to know about the young men and women you will be teaching, and they will know from day one that the classroom is for and reflects them. Keep the bulletin boards up for Fall Parents' Night of Classes or Open House or whatever your school schedules early in the school year.

ASSEMBLING A CLASSROOM LIBRARY

Begin building your classroom library by collecting new and used books right away. Many libraries have monthly book sales, and you can find books at reasonable costs. Visit garage and yard sales in your community. Invite graduates to donate books before they move on to the next stage in their lives. Ask relatives and friends to help. Some may be traveling and want to bring back something you can use.

Contact local service organizations like Kiwanis, Lions, and Rotary for contributions. Many such groups encourage support of educational endeavors. See titles to consider from those recommended by Goodreads on their website "Top 100 Middle School Must-Reads." Include picture books, too. They are particularly effective for creating interest and providing background information as you start a general unit or begin teaching a specific fiction or nonfiction text. Your school may qualify for programs such as that offered by bookmentors.org, a nonprofit, which uses micro-patronage, making donations to supply books for teachers, students, and librarians in high-needs schools.

Check business offices and hair salons with waiting rooms. Managers and owners welcome a dependable place to pass along old magazines when new ones arrive. (Of course, add to your library only those that are appropriate for students you teach.) Invite students to bring self-selected reading to class daily and then encourage them to pull out the magazine or book and read silently whenever they complete assignments before the period ends.

One of your most valuable teaching tools can be a classroom library stocked with books students can borrow, and with magazines they can read, scan, skim, and cut up for projects—but do not get too attached to these materials. Some will disappear but will be read by someone.

SCHMOOZING THE LIBRARIANS, MEDIA, AND TECH SPECIALISTS

Your librarians, media, and tech specialists can be your most precious human resources. These respected professional colleagues interact with teachers across the curriculum and with students from all grades; they know the curriculum very well. Moreover, librarians know their collection of materials and can work with you to utilize them in ways that support lessons with culturally relevant and age-appropriate selections.

As soon as you have an idea of what and when you plan to teach particular units, make an appointment to meet with your school librarian and media tech person. They may volunteer to reserve books, magazines, journals, and newspapers and identify online sites that students can use. Librarians are often willing to prepare a talk to introduce your students to media available in your school resource center.

Equally important, librarians usually know when the science and social studies teachers assign their big projects and can help you avoid student overload by recommending alternative due dates. It is good if you work at a school where those who teach the same grades work together to coordinate the scheduling of major assignments. It is better when there is interdisciplinary collaboration and a common project that students do for multiple classes with teachers from each class sharing grading. However, if that is not the case at your school, befriend the librarians and welcome the wealth of experience and knowledge they can add to your lesson planning and implementation.

Support in-class instruction with safe websites

PREPPING STUDENTS TO USE NEW
ELECTRONIC DEVICES AND PROGRAMS

It is easy to assume that students are already tech savvy and can easily use the equipment or the computer programs available at your school. But stop a minute: recall the small snags that frustrated you when you first used a new electronic device, a new computer program or application.

Check with the tech rep who can help you design lessons to show students efficient ways to navigate the technology available and give you some basic ways to troubleshoot problems when—not if—they arise. You can get off to a smoother start if you anticipate and prepare to address five basic steps. For students new to the school, you may need to help them learn

1. how to turn on the device,
2. how to log in using their school ID,
3. how to create a password (some schools have specific requirements for passwords),
4. how to navigate the specific program for doing their first assignment,

Prepare for a class demonstration during the second week of school with

- a protocol for assigning, picking up, or distributing the tablets or electronic devices.
- a class list with student school-assigned login names and general password.
- printed handout with steps to access the school portal leading to the program for just the first assignment. (Avoid overload and introduce other programs at a later date.)
- slides that demonstrate key steps for each of these tasks (save for later reviews).
- a short video tutorial that reviews the steps for using the program.
- screenshots showing what students should see on their devices when they get to specific steps in the program.
- a short assignment to complete during the class period. This could be sending you an e-mail with "HELLO from Period #" in the subject line and three things in the body of the e-mail they hope to learn this school year.
- a timer to ring ten minutes before class ends to allot time for students to log off and for you to collect and store equipment/devices for the next period.

Circulate and assist as needed. If you have students familiar with the technology, invite them to be teaching assistants for the day.

By preparing and accepting help, you can reduce the frustration of getting students online, into the school portal, and having a successful experience.

GUIDING PRINCIPLES TO MANAGE MAYHEM

Middle school students can be marvelous and mischievous. Think about ways to maximize the former and minimize the latter. Reflect on what you can and cannot stand in terms of classroom behavior, homework deadlines, movement and noise in the classroom, and flexibility in assignments. Prepare notes on how you will outline acceptable classroom behavior for your students.

Experienced teachers often have three or four general principles that can be applied in specific situations. Consider, as a start, those that refer to attendance, homework, and student behavior in class such as

- be present,
- be prepared, and
- participate courteously.

Once you decide your three or four guiding principles, include them on your class handouts, your website, the wall in your room, all major assignments, and in a letter to parents/guardians at the beginning of the school year. It is essential for all to know the basic principles by which you plan to conduct your class. It also is good for students to be reminded throughout the course. When they understand reasons for rules, students usually respond with compliance rather than adolescent sarcasm. Some schools have building-wide behavior statements and expect you to teach and follow them with little or no tweaking.

Assessing Prior Knowledge

Your students may be young adolescents or full adults, but none are new travelers along the road of life. They are joining you for just this portion of a lifelong journey of living and learning and are already familiar with experiences that can enhance your time together. As a teacher, fellow traveler, and tour guide, you want to do all you can to prepare them for the weeks and months ahead, perhaps warning them of possible landslides that can occur and inclement weather they may experience, always assuring them that you are all in this together.

You are there to help them climb the rock walls of new tasks that seem unscalable; to work with them, eager to observe them open their hearts and minds to see and appreciate the beauty of reading, writing, and discussing. You can help them think about new kinds of writing, novel narratives, and fascinating essays, ready-to-explore natural wonders encountered along the way. Most of all, you can guide their practice and use of skills as they strive to achieve their own personal goals.

You may find it helpful to use online resources to discover the range of learning styles among students you have in each class, on sites with online quizzes like "What's Your Learning Style?" Keep in mind that this information will provide just one component of the range of information you need to know about your students. You should also pay attention to their age, readiness, and interests.

You need to recognize what students already know and are able to do in the first couple of weeks. This could be collecting reading comprehension and writing samples, conducting interest surveys, or as described in chapter 2, observing small group activities during which students work together on a common project using skills they should be bringing to the new class.

Jazmen Moore, an early career teacher in her first semester at a new school, included questions like "What is your best memory connected to reading and/ or writing? Why? What is your worst memory connected to reading and/or writing? Why?" These questions provided useful feedback on how students felt about learning as well as a writing sample. Both helped guide her subsequent instruction.

Begin the school year the way you would like it to continue throughout the year. For example, consider homework deadlines. Be informative and firm from the beginning. Students understand that firm and fair do not mean inflexible. Most can deal with special circumstances, so do not be afraid to be merciful. It is normal to make adjustments as the school year unfolds. Beginning with a few general rules helps to establish groundwork for the upcoming year. In the metaphor of the school year as a trip, you are working on the rules for the road.

DECIDING RULES FOR THE ROAD

Among the rules, decide procedural matters like how you can organize and keep your lesson plans and master copies of handouts, as well as how you can collect and where to store student work. Consider using color coding as often as possible. For example, you could have different-colored loose-leaf binders for each grade or sturdy folders in assorted hues for each period. If you have access to colored paper for photocopying, you could use a single color for assignments in the same unit. It can be helpful to students if you were to say, "Sylvia, will you bring me the folder for your class? Yes, the purple one in the second shelf on the left corner of my desk," or to the class, "Take out the blue assignment sheet for our unit on poetry," or to Horace who's come for extra help, "Did you bring the yellow sheet with the academic vocabulary list?"

If you are really uncomfortable with lots of noise but understand the value of small group discussions, think about ways to design lessons that include specific

Circulate, observe, and assist as needed

instructions you explain ahead of time. It is helpful to write or project the daily-class outline and steps for assignments right on the board. Teach students to talk in their six-inch voices. When students know exactly what is expected and you are very present among them, they can usually discipline themselves enough to work in a focused manner and maintain a lower noise level.

Grading Guidelines

Just as you like knowing what is expected of you, the same is true for students. On a road trip, you look for signs indicating how close you are to your destination. When you see familiar topography or promised landmarks, you relax a bit and breathe a little easier. The same can be true about grading as it relates to you and your students.

Grading becomes less stressful when you understand what you are looking for in each assignment and share these expectations with students. They can review their work before turning it in, using your guidelines as a checklist. Some students, because of other commitments, may settle for a B rather than put in the time to earn the A. That's okay. It is their choice.

Fewer students challenge their grades when they have had a clearly written set of printed instructions to which they can refer before submitting their work. Consider a set of general grading principles that can be applied to most assignments. Explain these guidelines in the first couple of weeks, but not on the first day of school. Students will already be overwhelmed with the newness of everything! You can, however, have something like the following posted on your website and on any general handouts you distribute on opening day. (See figure 1.1.).

C = Complete (includes all components of the assignment)

B = Complete and Correct (minimal errors in mechanics, usage, grammar, and spelling)

A = Complete, Correct, and Creative (something original, fresh, special that enhances final paper, performance, or product)

Plan to include rubrics with each graded assignment, especially those that are weighted heavily enough to have major impact on reported grades. Providing students with a list of the standards and semester goals fulfills comparable purposes. Such information affords the same comfort as a map or the voice on a GPS when traveling in unfamiliar territory.

UNDERSTANDING BRAIN DEVELOPMENT AIDS IN LESSON PLANNING

New middle school teachers are often surprised at how literal their students are, especially in the earlier grades and as the school year begins. You may be

GENERAL GRADING GUIDELINES

A = complete, correct, and creative
B = complete and correct
C = complete
D = deficient (something missing)
F = failing, for now

C = THE SEA–*Complete* (include all components of the assignment)
B = THE BOAT–Complete and *correct* (rides on the sea with minimal errors in mechanics, usage, grammar, and spelling)
A = THE SAIL–Complete, correct, and *creative* (something over and beyond the boat; original and fresh elements enhancing the final written paper, performance, digital or art product)

Figure 1.1.   Share grading guidelines with students, parents, and administrators

disappointed that these young teenagers seem so very immature; few are able to see the subtleties in literature and appear inept at writing clever imagery. The fact is few young adolescents are mentally ready for this kind of thinking. No need to despair.

As the year unfolds, some students may display a leap in development of the brain's frontal cortex that occurs in early teens.[2] Others only get taller and wilder. At the beginning of the school year, young teens are usually still pretty literal, thinking in concrete terms, but as the year progresses and their frontal lobes mature, these youngsters begin looking at literature and life more abstractly, recognizing and using more subtle metaphors in their speech and writing. They are growing physically, emotionally, and cerebrally. Plan with this knowledge in mind.

IDENTIFYING RELUCTANT READERS EARLY IN THE SCHOOL YEAR

Unfortunately, there may be students in your classes who are not yet fluent, competent readers. You can be attentive to signals of unruly behaviors in students who may sit in the back, hoping to hide or who act the "clown," hoping to distract. Some appear to be indifferent or refuse to read out loud. Reading specialist Ellen Murray would remind you that reading out loud is a different skill than reading silently, and instead recommends watching out for reluctant readers who ask you to repeat yourself. They may be trying to memorize instructions because they are not confident they can read them. Such students may simply wait, looking around to see what classmates are doing before getting started on the assignment themselves.

The challenge for the school year is not to just identify reluctant readers but to help them overcome negative self-images that make them feel stupid, that it may be too late, or that they will never be able to read well. They offer a special challenge; these students will take great pains to hide this inability. Being alert and prepared, you can help each of them be more successful during this school year journey.

LEARNING THE LANGUAGE OF THE LAND

You know the value of a broad, rich vocabulary, even if you just visit a different area of the nation and not some exotic country on a different continent. The same is true for your students. For many of them, the language of school seems just as foreign. As you scope out the journey of the school year, you know students will need to understand some basic terms to be able to follow directions and stay on task. You can plan from the very beginning to teach vocabulary intentionally without having to drill students, just for them to acquire the skill of recognizing and using more sophisticated language in and out of class. If they use it, they won't lose it.

Consider levels of vocabulary. As you choose and prepare lessons around specific readings, first list and give definitions for words that are specific to that particular book/article, as well as some of the published academic vocabulary words that students will need to know across the content areas. You may recognize these levels as Tier 1, 2, and 3 vocabulary referring to the practical words used in everyday speaking, reading, writing, and academic use. You may know this as the 40/40/40 rule. Decide: What words do students need to know for forty days? for forty weeks? for forty years?—and then allot teaching and study time accordingly.

Think about dedicating space for a word wall so students see words daily during discrete units and can refer to and draw from this list when they write or talk about the topic or text. The wall list can be a poster to which you add words all through the school year or one that you change to coordinate with specific units of instruction. If space is limited, it may be better to have one permanent poster with general words and a changing posting with specific words. Fresh lists create new interest just as changing road signs you notice along the highway revive interest in the trip.

Teaching Test-Taking Language

Administering standardized tests will probably be part of your responsibility as leader of this educational expedition. Just as you find it comforting to know how to read the basic language of the land when you visit a foreign country, prepare your students to read signs that direct their work on a test. Teach your students the language of academic assessments long before students take these tests. Use such terms on assessments you give all year long.

Among the academic words to begin defining and using in early lessons are those having to do with instructions: explain, diagram, evaluate, describe, analyze, discuss, and so on. If your students are new to middle school or have been away from academic work for some time, they may have different ideas about what is required when asked to do these tasks. Help your travel-mates get off to a good start by clarifying what is expected when they see or hear these terms. You can find lists of academic words on websites describing Bloom's Taxonomy Verbs to help you measure students' level of knowledge, comprehension, application, analysis, synthesis, evaluation, and creativity.

Once you have settled into your classes, you may want to have a lesson on different definitions the same word may have in different content areas. Words like *plot* that in English is an element of fiction; in history/social studies, map reading *plot* of land or *plot* a course of action; and in science or math, *plot* a graph. "Draw," as seen in the earlier paragraph, is another of those multidefinition words.

Rewarding Language Learning

To speed up students' acquisition of vocabulary, encourage and reward them for using words from your vocabulary lists in the writing they do in other classes. A maximum of ten points per marking period—one point for each word in a graded assignment for other classes—should suffice. All extra credit work should be due one week before the end of a marking period to avoid last minute papers when you need time for computing grades to be submitted or posted for report cards.

Promote active learning by inviting students to bring in samples with the vocabulary words used in their reading outside of class. You could simply put up a blank poster board and ask students to bring in highlighted photocopies of passages from other published writing where students find words from current vocabulary lists (no duplicates from same source). If you keep it low key, this should not escalate into a contest but remain a way to raise awareness of language use outside their academic setting.

You also could set aside a day in class when students are asked to include correct use of vocabulary words in their conversation in pairs, small groups, or even full-class discussion. It could be great fun especially if you let peers give the feedback instead of you. This is another strategy that encourages close listening. You may recall days when you were studying a foreign language—say Spanish or French—and the teacher announced, "Hoy día, sólo se habla español aquí!" or "Aujourd'hui, seul le français est parlé ici!"

Rather than waiting for a test that measures the understanding of vocabulary, you may find it more effective to require the correct use of vocabulary from current lists in their writing assignments instead of spending time making up weekly quizzes. During journal writing, students can be asked to use words from the list in sentences that include definition, synonym or antonym, or some context clue to the word's meaning. They can work in pairs to "check" these writings. By the time students have an assignment to be graded, most students will be confident about using the vocabulary words. For full-length writing for the week or bi-week, students can then be required to incorporate vocabulary from recent lists.

KEEPING UP WITH LEARNING
WITHOUT OVER TESTING

Current education theories proclaim the value of conducting both formal and informal assessments all year long. Such measuring apprises both students

What skills are you preparing to teach and measure?

and teachers about what is learned and taught successfully. When and how one should test are the questions that arise for teachers new to the profession or new to teaching middle school students.

You have very definite content matter you are required to teach, and you are expected to guide the students across tempestuous seas to learn and show what they know about good writing, efficient reading, effective speaking, courteous listening, and skillful use of technology. It may be useful to work backward by asking yourself questions like these:

1. What specific skill am I trying to develop or measure in this assignment? Is it

   * how well students understand the text we've studied together?
   * how well they can show what they know about analyzing a character?
   * how well they can write an organized response in a timed setting?

2. What will I need to see in their work to know their level of understanding or skill? Is it

   * reference to the text?
   * correct use of literary language?
   * organization?
   * development of ideas?
   * correct use of vocabulary and grammar?

Some of these skills are revealed in student journal writing and conversations within small group and full-class discussion and may not need to be measured again on a formal test. As you become more experienced, you will design strategic lessons to measure student learning, become a more efficient listener, close observer, and develop the habit of taking brief notes based on what you see and hear during regular classes.

You may find it practical to write reflective journal notes at the end of each day. Doing so keeps you attuned to what students say, do not say, and how they respond and react. In the meantime, keep reading. A website like *Shared Space Planning* designed by Dr. Nicole Galante may help guide your planning.

You can become adept at using what you learn through formative assessments to reshape lessons, reteaching when necessary. This is like backtracking on a trip, a time when passengers notice details they may have missed the first time. In some situations, based primarily on informal assessments of student learning, you may speed up the pace and move on to the next unit of study. You know there could be potholes that may trip them up and quagmires that may bog them down; having extra time to negotiate them may be necessary. Still, you do not whiz on by. You take your teaching seriously, knowing you are more than a tour narrator who simply points out and names landmarks along the way.

Making formative assessments and deciding what to do about the results take practice. You may find it is like taking a break in the trip, checking the map, and assuring yourself that you have not drifted off the trail, distracted by the foggy, damp weather of students complaining that the terrain is just too rough! But the more proficient you become at recognizing learning and adjusting instruction, the less overwhelmed you and your students become at summative testing time. While both may be disappointed, neither the student nor the teacher should be surprised at the results of a formal test.

It's important to do what you can to ensure all those on the trip reach the destination safe, secure, confident, and competent with the knowledge and skills needed for continued success when you pass this tour group to the next year's tour guide.

PREPARING TO ASSESS FOR UNDERSTANDING

Test-taking skills are important for students to learn, especially as they prepare for more demanding courses in high school and beyond. You can serve your students well by reviewing those skills and then formatting tests in a student-friendly way. Your young or less-experienced students not only appreciate less-stressful testing but also perform better on assessments they understand. This can be as simple as creating a "Prepare for the Test" handout that includes the format and suggestions on how to study for each kind of question. Possessing a map that shows the topography of the hike can be comforting to a teen trekker.

For example, if you plan to test their understanding of vocabulary from the book, tell your students whether they need to know definitions, synonyms, antonyms, or how to use the words in a sentence. Or, if you have had students copy selected passages from the book into their reading journals, you should be able to test successfully for quotations simply by reminding students to study the text material in their journals.

If you have test questions that require answers in complete paragraphs or short essays, remind students in advance to review the structure of each one. A test prep handout can also include the number of points allotted for each test section. Such information saves time and angst. Students do not have to figure out the format of the exam or how best to allot their time. On the test-review day, remind students to focus on studying for sections with the highest value.

Your preparation of these handouts evokes reflection on what you have taught, what you are planning to measure, and whether this test will show student learning. With such thinking before the test, grading these assessments usually takes less time.

Keeping Records of Informal Assessments

Do you know any regular travelers who do not keep some kind of written, photo, or video record of their trip? Many more intrepid ones do all three. The same is true for you as teacher-tour guide. As you work with your students, offer different ways for them to show what they are learning, sometimes assessing with computer app quizzes, essays, art, music, drama, video, and inviting students to choose as often as appropriate.

Have students include in what they submit for evaluation a page explaining how their choice of product or performance will prove they know the content and have the skills required to meet the standards. Keep a checklist of the standards in each of their classroom folders so students can view them regularly.

You could schedule biweekly in-class reading days during which you meet with individuals for three to four minutes reviewing their progress for the week and plan for the next. It may be useful to plan meeting with half the class one week and the other half the next week. As students learn to draw from their wealth of knowledge and apply it in new situations, they become more competent and confident learners.

Teaching this way can create some uncertainty on your part, but with practice on both sides, your students will be more motivated and self-assured if they know where they are supposed to be by the end of the school year and have some choices in as many ways as are appropriate in your school. A tour guide knows the passengers need to eat and offers restaurant options within the framework of the time or budget. As you consider the full year, keeping an eye on the goal, you will see there is much room for flexibility and personalization in ways that lead to effective and efficient teaching and consistent, satisfactory learning.

RETEACHING IN DIFFERENT FORMATS

A fact of teaching is that students do not always treasure the pearls of wisdom that flow from your lips. They do not always remember exactly how to do everything you present them, even things they have previously done well. It is imperative to solidify that knowledge and hone those skills by asking students to use them in different settings. You can help increase retention by designing lessons that require your students to apply what they have learned from reading a short story or news article when they prepare a speech or write an essay.

For example, on Friday, you could ask students to choose a passage they particularly enjoy in their self-selected book and pattern that passage about something the student has recently experienced or observed. Then turn to a partner quietly and read the original passage aloud followed by their patterned writing. Ask students to pay attention to the sentences' rhythm. Then, listen closely to see how well their partner has followed the sentence syntax of the original writer. Exact duplication should not be required; coming close enough to show attentive reading and an attempt to pattern a published writer's style should suffice. Trust the students to know what works but circulate among them to confirm their analyses.

You could have students do scavenger hunts in their self-selected books, looking for whatever grammatical structure or reading strategy you have taught most recently. For example, ask them to find complex sentences; sentences written in passive or subjunctive voice; sentences using complementary conjunctions, reflecting different text structures, and so forth. How many different kinds of sentence starts do they notice on a single page? What does this suggest about interesting and effective writing?

Grading? Have groups check one another's work. Anything they cannot figure out together, discuss as a class. The teacher circulates, taking notes on level of participation, assessing informally, planning the next lessons, and continuing down the road, intent on completing the trip together.

INCORPORATING MOVEMENT, COLORS, AND SHAPES TO ENHANCE LEARNING

From your own experience traveling, you know how easy it is to get bored when you must sit a long time or when there is nothing interesting to see from the windows. As the leader of the educational journey, you can keep your charges engaged if you spice things up a bit with lessons that include movement, colors, and personal choices.

Learning Actively

Begin thinking about ways to incorporate kinesthetic games and active learning as a regular part of your instruction. Consider lessons that invite students to get up from their seats for reasons as simple as moving into groups or as sophisticated as expressing an opinion by the corner in which one chooses to stand. It will be like getting up and walking down the aisle while on a trans-Atlantic airplane trip. Sometimes you just have to get up and move. In the classroom, movement can lead to learning.

Do you have access to an LCD projector or digital camera and a whiteboard? If so, you can project games, puzzles, and diagrams onto the whiteboard. This way all students can see, but have to get up and write, draw, circle, or indicate a choice. Instead of worksheets students complete at their seats, you could project some on electronic slides or transparencies where students must walk up and write answers "on the board."

You can plan lessons where students have to express their opinions by getting up and going to a corner of the room to indicate their position on questions about literature or about life. For example, after reading about a choice the protagonist has made, ask students to go to a front or back corner depending on their opinions or predictions about the story: "What do you think Alfonso should or will do? Four different suppositions? OK, Sal and those who agree with him, stand over there. Those who think Hamera is right, stand with her, back there. Gerald, stand right here, and, Felicia, right there, and those who think their predictions are right, join them."

Ask each group to sit together and find evidence from the text to support their thinking. Choose a spokesperson to explain. Then having heard the evidence and reasons for opposing opinions, invite students who wish to change places to do so. Thinking, moving, talking, referring to texts, speaking, listening, moving, and learning = good teaching.

Using Shapes and Colors

Plan now to increase critical thinking and appeal to students who learn in different ways. Adapt lessons for visual and spatial learners to consider which color or shape is appropriate to add to something you projected. For example, some students may benefit from seeing the structure of an essay and how each part of it has a specific function. This works when you compare an essay to a train and have different geometric shapes represent different kinds of train cars:

- Right-facing triangle for the introduction: the engine—moves the essay forward

- Rectangles for the body: the cargo or box cars—containers carrying facts, explanations, and reasons
- Left-facing triangle for the conclusion: the caboose—looks back on what has been said
- Ovals: the couplings—these represent transitions that connect the parts of the essay

Use colors to show patterns of essay construction, with different organizational patterns for various paragraphs within the body of an essay. This visual activity can be done with photocopies of an essay. Students use colored pencils or markers to show the way parts of an essay should blend to explain, explore, and expand on the statement of purpose or thesis sentence. Some students probably already know that red and blue make purple, or blue and yellow make green. They can understand the concept of blending to create something new.

- Thesis statement in purple (or green)
- Topic sentences in red (or blue)
- Supporting sentences in blue (or yellow)

Seeing colors can also help students understand both the function of parts of speech and the impact of syntax on sentence structure when you ask them to circle, underline, and draw arrows as part of a grammar lesson. Use different colors for parts of speech or parts of the sentence. For example

- green for action verbs,
- brown for linking verbs,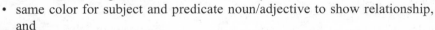
- same color for subject and predicate noun/adjective to show relationship, and
- dark color for noun/lighter version for pronoun to show agreement

Draw an arrow from the modifier (word, phrase, or clause) to the word modified. If there are dangling modifiers, students will see how out of place the dangler is.

Keep movement in the lesson by inviting students to work on sentences written or projected onto the whiteboard or on swaths of white butcher paper. You could project a sentence with a dangling modifier and have students draw what they "see" based on the wording of the sentence. If you have space in your room, you could have groups of students working on the floor with poster board and markers. There will be giggling, but that's OK. It releases tension.

Showing Patterns in Fiction

If students are not allowed to write in their books, print out or project a section from the exposition of a story you are teaching so all can see. Then invite one student at a time to come forward to mark on the projected passage, asking individuals to

- draw an oval around main characters when first introduced (different color for each one)
- underline in the matching color words/phrases that describe each of the main characters

  - Character A: Red. words describing him or her underlined in red
  - Character B: Blue. words describing him or her underlined in blue

- mark word(s) that identify the setting

  - Rectangle for place where story or scene is set
  - Circle for time of day, year, or period in life (childhood, teens, adult) the story is set

Just as noise and movement outside the window of a bus or train attracts the attention of travelers who may have dozed off, these verbal and visual activities capture students' attention and reengage them in lessons. They teach and reinforce concepts, showing students that fiction writers usually introduce main characters in stories early and very soon afterward include words and phrases to help shape images of characters and their personalities in the minds of readers.

Since the time and place of a story are often critical to the action, that information is also presented in the exposition. Seeing features together will remind students to look for these patterns when they read. Recognizing these expected literacy devices will help them as they begin writing stories of their own.

Sensing Surroundings as Sources for Writing

How about including time for side trips in your plans for this extended journey? Consider taking students outside to explore their environment as an alternative journal assignment. They can take notebooks or tablets, cell phones, and plastic grocery bags. Then have them write what they experience through their senses. You also carry your cell phone with timer app.

Depending on your school setting, this could simply mean finding a grassy area and asking students to sit on their grocery bags and close their eyes for two minutes; alternate between sensing and writing as they listen, smell, touch, taste, and then look. If your school permits students to have cell phones in class, students with a camera can take photos to add to journal entries. First sense, then write, and then photograph. (It helps to keep eyes closed as they experience the first two senses.)

- Close eyes for a couple of minutes and LISTEN, then write what they hear.
- Close eyes for a couple of minutes and INHALE deeply, paying attention to the different fragrances/odors/aromas; then describe them with vivid adjectives and figurative language.
- TOUCH—Pick up a stick and a rock and touch the bark of a tree, some pebbles, and a clump of soil. Describe that, or just how it feels to be sitting on the ground on top of a plastic grocery bag.
- TASTE—Bring along wrapped candy in different flavors and ask students to describe the taste sensation and the feel of the candy in their mouths, on their jaw, teeth, and tongue. Or bring a bag of those baby carrots, radishes, or celery sticks to have something healthier.
- SIGHT—Ask students to look around, paying attention to something they may not have noticed before, and describe it. (Save sight for last. By that time, students will have calmed down a bit and are ready to look at something other than one another.)

A change of place changes the pace

To make the excursion more active, you could have students walk around, stop, sense, write, and then walk to another spot. You also could have them do some gentle calisthenics—stretches, bends, twists—then sit and write as though they were a character in a story describing what that exercise felt like.

The notes from this outing can be used right away in poetry, or to flesh out a scene in a short narrative piece. You will have students who find it difficult to focus at each step in the lesson, which means saving this kind of adventure until you have established rapport and can depend on students to respond promptly with appropriate classroom behavior. In fact, this kind of outing can be a goal for you and a reward for them.

From the beginning of the school year, it helps to create and cultivate an environment in which the students feel comfortable writing personally. However, it takes time for students to trust you enough to do so. No need to give up. Writing about something done as a class may make them feel less vulnerable because it is a shared experience. This kind of side trip adventure may be just one way to scaffold writing where students begin writing fictionally but are encouraged to use their own experiences, lending authenticity to their writing, whether poetry, short story, or narrative essay.

If it is not realistic to take a local field trip outside the school building, obtain permission from the administrator and from the person in charge of the cafeteria, auditorium, theater, or library to schedule a field trip to those spaces. If you have several sections of the same class, you may end up taking different classes to different places depending on the weather, time of day, and places available. It is surprising what students notice when they tune in to experience a place through their senses.

While all these strategies do not require every student to be moving at the same time, what movement there is helps create and retain interest. Having to select colors and shapes gets them thinking. Sensing their space focuses their attention inward; writing and photography move thinking outward into the public realm. Those reading and viewing their classmates' notes and photos relive the experience from a different perspective.

Whatever you decide to do, it is important to create a safe and nurturing environment so students will not be reluctant to step up and show what they think they know. If they are wrong, they should not be embarrassed by anyone in the classroom. Invite them to share their journals and pictures. Being realistic, no one always pays attention. But if lessons are varied, vigorous and energizing, sometimes fun, and consistently supportive, more student travelers remain tuned in for longer periods of time throughout the journey.

No matter how engaging the intellectual outings you plan or enthusiastically they respond to the jaunts you schedule for this school year trip, you are responsible for seeing that your students attain the standards set for the course. Evaluation time comes, and students must be ready.

STAYING HEALTHY ALONG THE JOURNEY

Totally exhausted after a thoroughly exasperating week, you may begin to wonder, "How do great teachers stay on top of their game and retain the energy and enthusiasm to return to the classroom year after year?" Sipping a soothing cup of green tea, you ponder, "Why are so many long-term educators still healthy and happy, successful, and satisfied with their career choice?" Another sip. Ah, that's better.

The knot in your lower back may loosen a bit. A little calmer, a little less stressed, you smile and envision the faces of those experienced teachers whom you would call "great" and you even try to see yourself among their ranks. However, you glance at the stack of papers still to be graded and you sigh, "Never. Not me. Errrr. Not I!" Whatever.

Whether you are a novice or veteran, no matter how much time you give to school work, there always is more to be done. "How do they do it?" stays in the front of your mind. Myriad answers swirl as you pick up your pen or click open the file, readying yourself to get back to work. One reason may crystallize when you consider what you have observed over the years. Great teachers somehow manage to achieve personal/professional balance.

You are probably familiar with the idea of a Sabbath. True, Sabbath has religious connotations, but observing Sabbath is also an attitude toward work that schedules regular breaks. Plan now to rest regularly. Rest is not necessarily sitting with one's feet up, a cold drink in one hand and the TV remote in the other. It can be a brief respite from the demands of the classroom.

You may decide set aside at least one day a week to do no school work—a regular date night with your spouse, children, parent, or significant other. If you decide to take on an extracurricular assignment as a coach or club sponsor, you can still observe Sabbath by focusing attention on the team or club, not lesson preparation and paper grading. I coached and traveled with competitive speech teams for twelve years and learned to resist the temptation to take papers to grade. It is surprising how efficiently one can prepare for Monday, rested and refreshed! Try it!

Those colleagues whom you admire for their balanced lives participate in activities completely unrelated to the subject they teach. One may cultivate roses and enter them in the state fair; others may serve on church or community committees. Some take gourmet cooking classes. Some play in a chamber orchestra or sing in a community chorus. Like Langston Hughes, they "laugh/And eat well/ and grow strong." Will you?

CONCLUSION

In other words, as the instructional tour guide in charge of the educational journey, plan now to take some time off regularly, just for yourself. When you are a little more relaxed and have reliable and healthy ways to renew yourself, you will be able to tackle these challenges with much more energy and creativity. While you cannot automatically embed what you know into the hearts and minds of your students, you can inspire them to embrace new knowledge as you model doing the same.

And you, too, can enjoy the trip.

NOTES

1. William Arthur Ward, "Quotes about Teaching," National Education Association, 2012. https://www.brainyquote.com/quotes/william_arthur_ward_103463 (accessed August 24, 2018).
2. A collaboration of Cornell University, University of Rochester, and the NYS Center for School Safety, "Adolescent Brain Development," ACT for Youth Upstate Center of Excellence, May 2002. http://www.actforyouth.net/resources/rf/rf_brain_0502.pdf (accessed April 6, 2012).

Chapter 2

Networking Socially
at the Start of a School Year

Getting to know you, getting to know all about you.
Getting to like you, getting to hope you like me.[1]

—Oscar Hammerstein

Even in the age of electronic social networking, in-person relationships are the most meaningful for teachers and learners. The classroom itself is a "site" for social networking among increasingly diverse students and teachers. Twenty-first-century learning is grounded in social connections, and most standards for English language arts encourage developing such associations. The best way to nurture connections is to design low-tech interactions.

The following projects show how to get your eclectic, energetic students working together so you can assess how well they are already reading, writing, speaking, listening, and using technology. Equally, daily activities during the first weeks of school help your students get to know one another and you, both online and in the classroom. All will be useful as they begin to explore, explain, and express themselves on the journey to come.

The five-day collage-making activity is based on group and personal responses to a shared reading and works well with older students in more stable classes. The one- or two-day scavenger hunt using the course anthology is more fitting for shorter class periods during the first week. It works well with younger, less-experienced students like those who are new to the school or may be using a literature anthology for the first time. The assignment about names can work well with students of any age.

27

RESPONDING TO A SHARED READING:
SMALL-GROUP COLLAGE ON BOOK OR STORY

If your students have read an assigned book over the summer, you are in luck. You can use the opening days to have students work in small groups to make poster or digital collages that reflect various perspectives on their summer reading, measuring their recall or understanding of the elements of fiction.

If your students have not already read a common book, assign a short story to read silently or aloud together in class. You might ask for volunteers so you can begin to identify some of the eager or hesitant readers, keeping in mind it is fine to let students decline. Another option is to assign them a short story to read for homework. Sandra Cisneros' "Eleven" and Gary Soto's "Seventh Grade" are stories with which most students can identify.

In either case, think of the first week of language arts classes as the staging ground for the semester. As you get to know individual students, you can map out personalized approaches to general student activities. Personalized need not mean individualized; here it means drafting lessons that match closer to the personalities of the specific students assigned to you.

A collage is a design created from lots of words and pictures. When assembled on poster board, it reveals a message about the work of literature.

Get to know them in the first weeks

Each group is responsible for finding pictures and cutting out words and letters to create a collage focusing on one of the following: (1) Main characters, (2) Setting, (3) Plot, (4) Conflicts, (5) Themes, (6) Literary devices. The collage can be prepared on poster board or created digitally using photos, clip art, and graphics students locate online. If technology is available to do it efficiently, students could take photos and upload and integrate them into their collages. Survey the skills and release students to choose as often as seems appropriate. Showing the timeline helps students decide which option to select.

The idea here is to get students involved in an activity that enables them to get to know one another and enables you to get to know each of them. Assemble the following:

1. scissors
2. glue sticks
3. poster board
4. magazines
5. colored markers
6. envelopes
7. access to enough computers for a least one per group
8. index cards
9. an electronic or kitchen timer
10. blank sheets of address labels (e.g., Avery 5160)
11. a clipboard

These lessons are designed for a fifty-minute class period, but you can adapt them as needed to fit your schedule. See textbox 2.1 for sample of collage assignment. If your students have ready access to electronic devices, you could assign students to create a brief movie from still shots or slides created in Prezi or PowerPoint programs and then show them during the oral presentation at the end. The key is time management and student skills to complete in a timely fashion.

Day One: Groups Conceive Their Collages

Students need instructions, especially on the first few days of class! They want to know what is expected. Therefore, project or post instructions somewhere in the classroom where everybody can refer to them, and print out a copy for each student if it does not overly clutter their desks or work surface. Inform students that while they are working together, you may be roaming around the room, listening in, observing, and enjoying their conversations. Inform them that there are no "right" or "wrong" answers, just courteous ones and text-supported ones.

Finally, before they begin working, distribute name tags—or tags for them to write their own names with markers, perhaps color-coded to indicate their group. Set a visible timer to ring ten minutes before the class period ends so you have time to collect supplies, clear up the room, reflect on what they have been doing, and give assignment for the next class meeting.

Once groups begin working, it is time for you to begin observing and listening. A clipboard and mailing labels are for you to jot down notes about specific students. If possible, write words on each label that students say during group activities. Listen for their pithy comments, not lengthy quotations. Jot down particular words, phrases, or short sentences that can help you to structure future lessons. Note whether students understand and use literary terms or synonyms that make sense. Indicate positive/negative language toward group members. For example, "You've got that right, Lindsay." "You dummy! Don't you know what conflict means in a story?"

Also, make short notes about the students. Who is talkative? Who is articulate? Pensive? Easily distracted? Who is having the most fun? Who likes asking tough questions? How are the various groups and members "doing" in their groups: forming, storming, norming, or by the end of the allotted time, performing as described in group dynamics research by Bruce Tuckman? Who is involved in these group-related activities? Be open and helpful. Define the literary terms as needed. Answer students' questions about the assignment. But avoid looking like a mere disciplinarian. Smile!

The timer is visual as well as aural. It can help get you and the students into the rhythm of time-crunched class sessions. Students, right at the beginning of the school year, need to start thinking about completing projects by deadline. So do you. The classroom needs to be cleaned up on time, especially if a colleague teaches in the same room after your class. The buzzer will signal time for cleanup. Tell your students that when a timer goes off at the end of class you need their help in straightening the room so that they can mess it up the next day. They smile!

At the end of class, ask students to bring in pictures—from magazines or printed out from websites—that can be used to represent people, places, events, conflict, and literary devices in their story. Be sure that you have your own supply on hand for those unable to bring pictures or magazines to the next class meeting. For those who have access to Internet at home, encourage them to search, saving images onto a site the students can access from school. If the group is making a poster, the students may choose to print out the pictures and bring them to the next class meeting.

Day Two: Groups Compose Their Collages

Briefly repeat instructions for the assignment, tell students how long they have to create a layout for their collages, and set a timer to signal the last ten minutes for cleanup. Since some of the collages are not likely to be finished, provide envelopes for groups to store their unused pictures. Remind those working online to save their work on the class website you have set up.

Invariably, during this second class meeting, some groups wish they had the images that other groups are using or discarding. If day one was not overly chaotic, encourage covetous groups to swap some pictures, being careful that cross-group racket does replace intra-group collaboration. You can always institute a couple of one-minute swap sessions to limit as well as encourage picture-trading—call it "Picture Jeopardy." Play the theme song while students make changes. Once the music stops swapping ends, and groups return to work with pictures they have on hand.

Next, begin testing the validity of your observations about students from the previous day. See if behavior you observed the first day continues, changes, improves, or devolves. Also start looking for additional information about your crew. Who comes prepared? Who acts like the "artistic coordinator?"

Groups meet wherever comfortable and productive

Which students seem more concrete or philosophical in group discussions? Who encourages group members who may have been on the periphery of the discussions? Does anyone seem overwhelmed, suggesting that you might need to provide additional encouragement and support as they board the ship for another school year? Remember to jot down brief comments by individual students, such as "Can't you do anything right?" and "I like that picture."

Day Three: Groups Complete Their Collages

By now, students are wondering what they have gotten themselves into— through no choice of their own! They might be wondering if this class is going to be a lot of fun as well as a lot of work. It is time for all of you to face the reality of school deadlines, including those for collaborative work. Students must demonstrate what they have learned. So, keep smiling but also start acting like the benevolent taskmaster you really are.

First, project the assignment so they see and can refresh their memories. Tell them that the collages must be completed that day. Finally, joyfully deliver the news that during the next class meeting, the groups are to give oral presentations based on their collages—and that each student is expected to contribute. Even your overachieving groups with already-completed collages now have plenty to do. A few of your students might be thinking uncomplimentary thoughts about school and especially about you. As Huckleberry Finn put it, "All I say is, [teachers] is [teachers], and you got to make allowances. Take them all around; they're a mighty ornery lot. It's the way they're raised."[2]

Hand each student a 3 × 5 index card. Inform the class that each group should jot down a couple of comments answering questions about its collage, such as "What does a particular image or group of pictures signify to them with respect to the story?" and "What does the collage reflect about different parts of the reading?" Again, emphasize that there are no right or wrong answers. These presentations are not graded. Stress the fact that you are looking for creative responses to the reading. After all, this is language arts.

Undoubtedly, a few students become preoccupied with the stressful fact that they must make an oral presentation on the fourth day of class when they are still anxious about relationships with their classmates and teacher. Some students are relieved to know that they get to present in groups. Remind them that they can refer to notes on their index cards. Even just a few key words or phrases should help each student follow through with his or her part of the presentation.

Day Four: Students Individually Convey Their Group's Thoughts

Allot ten or fifteen minutes at the beginning of class for groups to meet briefly to determine their intra-group speaking order and recall what each member will say on behalf of the group. Ask a member of each group to write the speaking order on the class board so that everyone can see when to present.

To support smooth transitions between presentations, have students arrange the poster boards on the chalk or marker tray in the order of the presentations, but with posters facing away from the audience. When group members rise to share their collage, one can turn their board to face the audience. When the group finishes,

---

TEXTBOX 2.1:   GROUP COLLAGE

Preparation

Note the specific tasks for each literary feature or trait and be prepared to explain reasons for choices.

- *Setting*: Choose five or six significant settings. Represent the settings in terms of the impact each has on the main character; consider also the connection of the various settings with the title of the story.
- *Characters*: Choose five or six important characters. Present or depict them in terms of their relationship with main character and the significance of their influence upon that protagonist.
- *Conflicts*: Choose five or six memorable conflicts in the story. Depict the characters involved in each conflict as well as the effect the conflict has on the protagonist as a participant or observer.
- *Symbolism and Figurative Language*: Select examples of five or six particularly effective devices (symbols, images, metaphors, figures of speech) the author uses to illustrate character, conflict, or theme or to unify the story.
- *Lessons Learned*: Put yourselves in protagonist's shoes. Identify three or four of the most important lessons that you think that character learns and, perhaps, benefits from those experiences. These lessons may be supported by any of the previous elements: setting, characterization, conflict, use of symbolism, and figurative language.

Presentation

Plan a six- to seven-minute presentation during which your group displays and explains your collage. All group members should speak about equal time. Plan the order each member is to speak, using notes, but not read word for word. Decide where each group member should stand so that the whole class can see the collage as you make your presentation. Practice what you plan to say, then you can establish and maintain eye contact with members of the audience. If your group makes a digital collage, be sure to save and send a copy to the teacher the evening before your presentation day.

the board turner should place their board behind all the others. For digitized presentations, have all files open so students only have to toggle to open their files.

If the room has space, invite class members to sit on the floor close to the collages so they can see more details. In most cases, individual pictures are too small for most to see clearly if all remain in their seats. For now, smaller than optimal collage details are acceptable since the primary purpose of making these posters is the opportunities for students to work together and for you to know more about them, rather than requiring polished speeches with equally professional-looking visual aids.

After the presentations, you can display the poster boards for a few weeks giving group members more opportunities to examine other groups' posters up-close. If the resources are available and the classroom is equipped, digitally photograph each collage and project the resulting images on a screen on Day Five or to show other classes who have a similar assignment. The digital photos also could be posted on your class website for families to view at home.

Day Five: Students Individually Compose Their Reflections

At the beginning of class, with the group posters displayed or projected onto the screen, ask the students to prepare a short, handwritten reflection about their experience in class during the first four days. While you take attendance and review your label-notes about students—associating your notes with their faces—they can be writing their first journal entries. They get to metacognate (think about) their responses to the collage-creating experience. Here are sample prompts.

- What did you have to consider about your story before creating a collage?
- How did you decide which picture worked better than others for your collage?
- Why did your group organize pictures and words as you did?
- What would you have done differently if you had been working alone?
- Do you think this is a useful activity to start the year? Why? Why not?
- What did you learn about yourself as you worked on this collage?
- What did you discover about your reading skills while working on this collage?

Ask students to write neatly while assuring them that their personal reflections will not be graded like exams or evaluated as formal papers. Then collect and simply read the journals, thinking about what they have written about the experience and what you learned as you observed them working together. These reflections are now baseline writing samples—not for grading, but for future comparisons along with additional samples forthcoming in students' journals. You also have examples of their handwriting to decipher!

SCAVENGER HUNTING IN THE COURSE ANTHOLOGY

Most students are oblivious to the vast resources available in language arts anthologies. Some students are unaware that an anthology is a treasured collection of texts—literary passages and art work—similar in language to the idea of a collection of flowers.

As you explain the concept of anthology to your students, ask them to picture a bouquet of a variety of beautiful, fragrant flowers. If you have access to a variety of fresh-cut flowers, bring them in a vase and label it "anthology." If not, simply project a lovely bouquet of familiar intermixed with exotic flowers. Meanwhile, ask students to prepare for a scavenger hunt inside their anthology. They are likely to look at you askance. That is simply curiosity and is just what you want to create.

It is best to avoid pressing students into feedback about the various social, ethnic, and national groups represented in the book. No anthology is completely diverse or thoroughly unbiased. Focus on the resources available in your collection rather than on its deficits.

PLANNING THE HUNT FOR PAIRS OF STUDENTS

If the publisher does not include a scavenger hunt among its resources, no need to worry. You can easily prepare fifteen to twenty questions to help students know where to find various elements—using the helpful journalistic method of asking the five Ws and an H (who, what, when, where, why, and how). If this is your first time using this textbook, you may be surprised at how much you learn yourself. Here are helpful categories:

General Content

1. Who is the author, editor(s), or publisher (explain the difference)?
2. What does the title mean or suggest about the contents?
3. When was it published—and when were various pieces written?
4. Where is the table of contents? How is it organized?
5. Where is the index? How is it organized—and why?

Graphics and Graphic Design

1. What is on the cover? Does it make the book seem interesting? Inviting?
2. Is there an introduction? If so, what is in it? Are the introductory pages in Roman or Arabic numbers (iii or 3)?

3. What kinds of design elements or text features are included (subheadings, captions, lines, colors, textboxes, maps, drawings, and photos)?
4. Is the artwork acknowledged? Ask students to find the name of the artist of a particularly interesting piece of artwork. (This information may be found in a separate index or simply identified in a special font within the anthology's complete index.)

Organization

1. How is the table of contents organized? Genre (category of artistic composition, similar to types of flowers, like roses), theme, time, nation, or country? Chronologically? Other?
2. Use the table of contents to find an author whose name begins with the letter of one of student's names. Is it a short story, a poem, and a play?
3. Use the index. What short story titles include words beginning with letters of your first name and your partner's last name?
4. How is each literary work introduced? (Devise a question that sends the students to this reader aid). Some anthologies include background information on the author, historical period, genre, or literary devices featured in the stories, poems, essays, or play(s).
5. Where in the book is information about authors of individual works or the editors of the anthology? (Send the students to a page to learn something unique about an author whose work you may teach later in the school year).
6. Does the anthology have questions following the text of each literary work, after several related pieces, or at the end of a unit? Send students to one such page and ask them to list the kind of questions found there—such as facts or interpretive responses, maybe even connecting the literature to their own lives.
7. Does this anthology include vocabulary and grammar links to websites? On what page(s)?

Supplementary Resources

1. If there is a glossary of literary terms, ask students to locate and read the definition of a term that may be new to them but that you plan to teach during the year—for example, onomatopoeia, pantoum, or limerick. Middle school students like the unusual sounds of these words.
2. Does the anthology define vocabulary? If so, ask students to find the definition of an interesting new word—maybe in a story they may soon read.
3. Is vocabulary defined in footnotes or side notes? If so, devise a question that requires students to use this text feature.

4. Does the anthology include grammar or writing resources—why or why not? (Question: Why would the publisher put such resources in a book about literature instead of in a book about writing?)
5. Are there lists of suggested readings? Website links? Other resource references?

Time to go hunting. Now the student pairs can explore the book for answers to the questions and then list three to four literary works they hope the class will study during the year. Circulate, listen, and learn.

As you hear them talking about what they notice in the book and note the selections they mention, you begin to sense what interests them. When possible, modify your lessons to include works that seem to draw their attention. Each pair of students can also develop a couple challenging scavenger questions to stump other classmates once the preliminary worksheet is completed.

If students take their textbooks home, assign the last question as homework. This gives your students a reason to review the book on their own and possibly introduce the book to parents or guardians. You might even ask students to show their book to other family members and ask which pieces of literature they have read or would like to read.

CELEBRATING NAMES

Asking students to learn and talk about their names is another engaging and insightful way to start to the school year, even for students who know each other well. This assignment has students conduct interviews and simple research, and then describe what they have experienced living with their names. Students of any age tend to respond enthusiastically to the task. Why? Because it is all about them.

One educator, Dr. Kalpana Iyengar, adapted the assignment to have pairs interview one another, spending a couple of days researching what they learn about their names and then preparing and giving oral presentations. She sparked their interests with readings and video clips about names. Two texts relatively easy to access are "My Name" from Sandra Cisneros' autobiographical novel, *A House on Mango Street*, in which she describes what it is like to carry her grandmother's name, and "Hidden Name Complex Fate," an essay by Ralph Waldo Ellison in which he discusses his experiences having been named for a famous intellectual. Choose the text(s) and video clips, like the one of Ms. Cisneros reading "My Name" that are most accessible to your students, and write along with them, telling about what it is like to live with your name(s).

Dr. Iyengar remarked that her preservice teachers talked about ways they would adapt this assignment to have their students draw original pictures and assemble a decoupage of family photos illustrating their written texts. Most agree that getting students involved with art and writing at the same time would make it a "funner" activity. Feel free to adapt the assignment to fit your students and purpose for giving the task.

To help students comfortably share their stories, after reading "My Name" by Sandra Cisneros and underlining phrases and sentences that catch their attention, ask the students to do a "quick write" based on a phrase or sentence they select from the vignette. A "quick write" is short, nonstop writing on an assigned topic; for a brief spurt of time, students let their thoughts flow without censoring them.

Ask students to copy an underlined phrase or sentence from the reading. Then use that phrase or sentence as a jumping off point to write rapidly about their own names for six or seven minutes. Write along with them and share with your students. The following is a sample quick write based on the Cisneros piece:

A PERSONAL STORY

"My Name"—A Quick Write Inspired by Sandra Cisnero's Vignette of the Same Name

Anna Jamar Small Roseboro. Is this "me?" My name is a combination of my paternal grandmother's, Anna; my maternal grandmother's, Jamie; my dad's name, Small; and my husband's name, Roseboro. Everyone has had my name—made something of it, then passed it along to me. Anna means "gift of God." Is it I who am the gift or my grandmother who is a gift to me? Jamie is short for Jamar. My grandmother, whose full name is Jamar Elna, is named for her four aunts, Jane, Martha, Ellen, and Nora—what a burden, what a privilege, to carry the names of so many relatives. Or is it a blessing? Am I standing on the shoulders of those who've come before me?

Small, my maiden name always caused me trouble. "Small," they'd tease. "You're not small; you're tall!" I was always the tallest girl in my elementary school classes. In high school, however, I used the name to my advantage. I ran for a senior class office. My slogan was "Good things come in Small packages." Finally, success with that name.

Then, I married Bill Roseboro during the years that Johnny Roseboro was a star catcher for the L.A. Dodgers. He'd been in the news because of a fight with Juan Marichal. Everywhere I went, "Are you related to Johnny Roseboro?"

"Yes, but what has that to do with me?"

Who am I really?

WRITING ABOUT NAMES

Early in the school year, keep it simple and just ask students to learn answers to as many of these questions as they can.

1. Use a dictionary or online resources to find out what each of your own names means.
2. Interview a family member to learn the sources of your name(s). If you have equipment, audio or videotape the interview. Who named you and why? Are you named for a friend or family member? Someone else?
3. Determine the kind of surname or last name you have. Is it a place name, like Al-Fassi, Hall or Rivera; an occupation, like Chandler, Smith, or Taylor; a descriptive, Braun or Strong, or a patronymic or version of a father's name, like Ben-Yehuda, McNeil, or Von Wilhelm, and so on?
4. Describe incidents you have experienced because of your name, including mispronunciations, misspellings, and misunderstandings.
5. Write about nicknames and related embarrassing or humorous experiences.
6. Identify challenges you feel because of the name(s) you carry.

As students consider responses to these prompts, they reflect on who they are in their families, the school, the wider community, and perhaps even the world. Some students may learn family history never previously discussed. Other students awaken tender memories of relatives and family friends for whom they have been named. Some may just be embarrassed; others pleasantly surprised. Sharing these stories brings a class together into a community ready to learn together on this school year journey.

CONCLUSION

Finally, end the first week of class meetings by reviewing with your fellow crew members some of your personal objectives for the year that may include

- increasing their appreciation, understanding, and enjoyment of reading;
- improving their understanding and use of the writing process;
- helping them become more at ease when speaking in front of a group;
- helping them increase their knowledge and use of sophisticated vocabulary;
- reviewing and extending their knowledge of correct grammar; and
- discovering more ways online resources can help them learn.

Keep in mind that the first week of class needs to be both task oriented and relational. While introducing students to the work, be sure to help introduce them to each other and to you.

Middle school students are some of the most creative people on the planet. Half of your job is to keep from squelching their bubbling personalities and literary imaginations. Older students may be more self-conscious, but all love using language to express themselves. They especially enjoy telling stories. They have probably been telling their families and friends stories about you and your class. Now you get to tell them about how stories work. That is the focus of the next chapters.

NOTES

1. Oscar Hammerstein, "Getting to Know You." Sound Track Lyrics. http://www.stlyrics.com/lyrics/thekingandi/gettingtoknowyou.htm (accessed April 2, 2012).
2. Mark Twain, *Huckleberry Finn*. https://www.gutenberg.org/files/76/76-h/76-h.htm (accessed August 24, 2018).

Chapter 3

Unpacking the Story and Understanding Genres

The best of my English teachers taught us literature because they wanted the art of it to expand our minds and help teach us new ways of seeing the world. I was taught to both see a work of literature as a way to understand the time it was written, and the people who produced it, and to find the parts of that work that spoke to me in my time and place.[1]

—Sybylla Yeoman Hendrix

This chapter explains how to introduce or review with students the basic elements of fiction by reading stories, analyzing plot structures and characterization, and eventually coaching them in composing their own short story to submit to a school journal or publish online. Notice that the approaches work well teaching short stories, novels, poetry, and plays. But equally know that as students learn the language of literature and come to appreciate how the elements work to construct stories, your journey-mates also come to see themselves and the world in new ways.

In much the same way that veteran world travelers learn some basic words and phrases for countries they will visit, enabling them to read signs and navigate in new territory and enjoy the trip, your challenge is to teach the language of literature without diluting that appreciation. Similarly, as a professional you know you must also develop and present lessons that help your students meet school, district, or state standards for the English language arts that include close reading, making logical inferences, citing specific textual evidence in speaking and writing to support conclusions drawn from the text.

INTRODUCING THE ELEMENTS

Here is a way to get your middle school students started and other students revived. They need a journal, like a spiral notebook or an electronic device, to which they have daily access. This study aid should be taken home daily, but if more appropriate for your setting, set up boxes or bins and store on classroom shelves. Then students can pick up their journals at the beginning of each class and return them at the end.

To help maintain order, label the bins or boxes with the class period number and sections of alphabet. If students have daily access to classroom computers, help the youngsters set up electronic files and folders they can access easily. It is helpful to establish a routine by the second week of school for picking up and returning notebooks and tablets. Make it a habit that works smoothly. Set your timer to allow five to seven minutes at the end of class. Then you can close in an orderly way, returning books and tablets, and reminding students of plans for next class meeting.

Show students the link on the school server or Internet sites you have vetted for preteen use that connects them to a safe place to save their files and access them in class, on the school site, or at home. It is critical to allot class time to review these sites early in the school year. If necessary, invite someone from the tech department to walk the class through the steps, answering questions early on, so you lose no class time later fumbling with equipment purchased to enhance, not inhibit, learning.

Ask students to set up their own journal section for short stories by folding a page in half vertically, forming a half-page bookmark titled "short stories" or creating a digital folder for this purpose. So begins their own story in this unit—opening their files or turning of their page (Not a bad metaphor!). Every new life story is a chance to begin again.

Have students write on the next clean page in their journals the current date in the upper right-hand corner, and as you introduce them, the elements of fiction on the top line. Remind the students that all writers start with blank pages even if they use computers. Few students ever think about the fact that most of what they read for your class was first written on paper, typed on a typewriter, or drafted on a computer.

Next, point out that writers use proven techniques to engage readers—just as musicians use notes, chords, and rhythms. Authors who wish to be published do not just write to quickly express themselves—like texters or bloggers may. Knowing the different facets of fiction helps writers write and readers read. In fact, understanding the structure of literature can assist in all kinds of human communication, from interviewing for a job to making a movie.

If you are comfortable doing it, start this unit on unpacking stories by telling your own story about something that happened in your life—something students may find humorous, unusual, or particularly revealing about you. Be a bit transparent to engage them. Then ask a couple of students if they like listening more to stories or lectures. Students usually admit that they like listening to stories more than lectures. Moreover, they acknowledge that they prefer lectures that use stories to illustrate points, rather than lectures that just spew facts. Hmmm.

Normally, it is best to teach those literary terms covered in your student textbook. If the text does not define terms, you can use the ones below or write your own. If you would like a refresher on some of the different definitions, use online sites for different definitions and a brief history of each term.

Consider assigning students several stories to read quickly, since multiple examples can be more effective than one. Below are ways of teaching each of the basic elements of fiction and suggestions to return to stories read earlier as you introduce new terms.

You may decide to do a pretest to discover what terms students already know. Simply create a list of terms students are expected to know by the end of the school year. Distribute the list and ask them to put a star next to terms they know and could explain, a check next to those they recognize, and a minus sign next to completely new terms.

As students are marking the lists, circulate peeking over shoulders to see if you notice a pattern among terms starred and checked. Allot time to have students turn and talk to a partner, explaining the words they starred and their

Teaching is more than telling

partner checked. Again, listen as they talk. By this time, students realize that they have more knowledge than they imagined but still have much to learn. Commend them for their candid responses and helpful conversations. Collect their lists, tally the results, and decide how best to use this formative assessment to adjust upcoming lessons.

Remember, it is always appropriate to review, so if students already know many of the basic terms, you may speed up the pace of lessons that follow. Or, assign the book report or project at the end of this chapter; allot a class period to visit the library to locate and check out books and in-class time to read them. Sometimes a special side trip during a tour is just the thing to re-energize those committed to a long trip. These self-selected books also provide fine fodder for feeding their minds, expanding their understanding about ways authors use literary devices, and samples for writing their own stories.

The sample lessons here follow the same basic order:

- Teach or demonstrate the term (an element of fiction or text structure)
- Assign a story or essay that clearly illustrates the term
- Encourage students to pay attention to how the story or essay reflects the element(s)
- Invite students to read for fun, so they do not focus so much on identifying the elements that they fail to enjoy the story or essay

Lesson One: Plot

1. Ask students to turn to the short story section of their journals. Explain that stories are about characters faced with solving a problem, confronting a conflict. The first term, *plot or narrative arc*, is the series of events that make up a story. Plot usually includes six parts: an exposition, triggering action, rising action, climax, falling action, and resolution.
2. Draw a diagram of a plotline on the board; use one prepared on a poster or electronic slide where all can see a diagram similar to the one in figure 3.1.
3. Fill in the six parts of the plotline as you explain the purpose of each one:

   - *Exposition*: Introduces the main characters, the setting, the conflict, and the point of view. (Ex = out, position = places, Exposition = places out for the reader . . .)
   - *Triggering action*: That story point when the main character decides to do something about the problem introduced in the exposition.
   - *Rising action*: A series of events during which the main character attempts to solve the problem introduced in the exposition. Usually, there are three attempts:

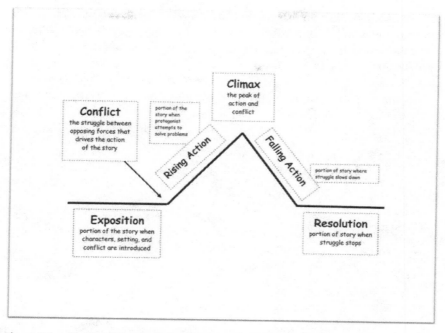

Figure 3.1. Plotline helps students visualize structure of fiction

- the first is very simple and performed alone;
- the second is more difficult, often requiring the help of another character; and
- the third is most complex, often requiring the main character to make a moral or ethical decision.

- If students are familiar with classic fairy tales, ask them to consider how often this three-part rising action occurs: "Three Little Pigs," "Goldilocks and the Three Bears," "Three Billy Goat's Gruff," and so on. Ask for examples of stories which may be more familiar in their culture or language; consider storylines from movies or TV shows.
- *Climax*: The highest point of suspense in the story, when the reader, viewer, or listener wonders whether the main character has gotten into such trouble that he or she cannot get out. Then the turning point occurs and the reader can see that the problem can be solved or (tragically) that the character has given up or been permanently overcome.

- *Falling Action*: The issues raised during the rising action begin to fall into place, the complications of the rising action seem to unravel, and the action begins to wind down. Some texts call this the dénouement (day-noo-mon).
- *Resolution*: The action stops and the readers see that the main character either has solved the problem or given up (not all stories have happy endings).

Close the session with the reading assignment, asking students to identify the narrative arc and plot parts in the story. Encourage those who wish to do so to draw and label the plot line in their journals. If you are teaching with block-scheduling, you can use the additional time to start or complete a short story so students can begin identifying parts of the plot.

Reading a story aloud and asking students to raise their hands when they recognize an element is a way to focus their attention on the elements and can serve as a no-stress assessment to determine whether they "get it." Be sure to stop reading at a critical plot point to entice the students to continue reading just to find out what happens next.

Lesson Two: Conflict

In fiction, conflict is the problem the main character(s) must resolve in a struggle against opposing forces. The main character may face internal conflict—a struggle for dominance between two elements within a person—or external conflict or conflict against an outside force—often both.

Once you introduce the topic of conflict, students should be ready to work in pairs for ten minutes identifying plot elements in the story they have just read. They can work together, referring to the definitions that they wrote in their notebooks and identifying specific examples from the text. Since sharing desk space is a psychological reminder to students that they are sharing what they are learning, it is appropriate to encourage the students to collaborate by pulling their desks together and talking with one another. Circulate during discussions to learn:

- what students recall about the previous day's lesson and from the story they just read;
- what needs to be retaught or clarified before continuing the lesson; and
- who has and has not done the homework.

Next, lead a classroom discussion of student conclusions for about fifteen minutes. Ask students to identify the conflict in the story just completed and reply using P.I.E. response structure—make the *point*, *illustrate* it with examples from the literature, and then *explain* the link between the illustration and the point.

Students can follow this pattern in their responses:

- State their opinion: "I think the climax of 'The Three Little Pigs' is when the wolf comes down the chimney."
- Support their opinion with an example from the text: "On page three, it says, 'Finally, the wolf got so hungry that he jumped down the chimney.'"
- Explain how the chosen passage illustrates the definition of the term: "This seems like the high point of the story because the reader really wonders if the pigs will be okay. Also, the action of the story starts to fall after this event."

Students use "because" statements to clarify their answer, illustrate it with an example from the text, and explain why that example fits the definition of the term they have just studied. Insisting on P.I.E. may slow down the rate of responses but necessitates deeper thinking. Requiring it allows time for those who process information more slowly time to do so.

Early in the school year, combining THINK/PAIR/SHARE with P.I.E. works well. Pose or post the prompt. Allot time for students to *think*, consult text, jot down notes before *pairing* with a partner or talking quietly with table-mates, then *sharing* in full-class discussion. This discussion/response format reveals to students that there is often more than one right response to a question, especially in the study of literature. Also, it allows you to determine students' understanding of the material and readiness for formal

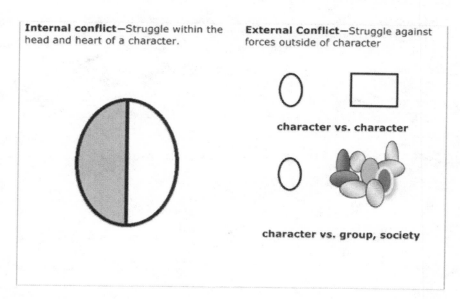

Internal conflict—Struggle within the head and heart of a character.

External Conflict—Struggle against forces outside of character

character vs. character

character vs. group, society

Conflict may be internal, external, or both

assessment. Finally, this format is excellent practice for writing fully developed essays.

Internal conflict occurs when a character struggles within himself or herself to decide what is the right, moral, or safe action. It is something like the cartoon devil and angel sitting on opposite shoulders of a character, trying to persuade the character to take certain actions.

External conflict occurs when the main character struggles against forces outside of himself or herself. The students may be surprised when reminded that even an animal or alien protagonist demonstrates a human-like struggle. Examples of external conflict include:

- person versus person—when the struggle is with another character;
- person versus nature—when the struggle is against a force of nature— weather, thirst, illness, or topography (desert, mountain, roiling rapids);
- person versus society—when the struggle is against a group of people acting as one—a team, racial group, pack of peers, political party, social club, ethnic tribe, and so on;
- person versus technology—when the struggle is against a machine, like a car, tractor, tank, android, or computer as may occur in natural or in science fiction; and
- person versus the supernatural—when the struggle is against a ghost, an alien, the gods, or a Supreme Being.

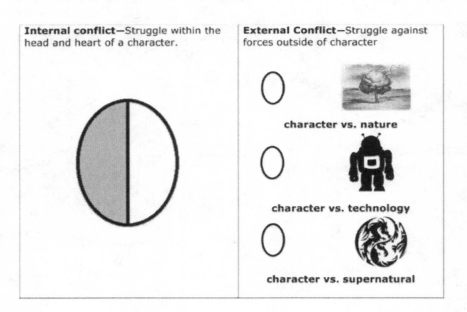

Internal conflict—Struggle within the head and heart of a character.

External Conflict—Struggle against forces outside of character

character vs. nature

character vs. technology

character vs. supernatural

Assign another short story to read for homework. If time permits, read aloud the opening passages. This is often enough to get students hooked and more likely to complete the reading on their own. Ask them to draw a plot line that represents the relative length of time it takes for each section of the story to unfold. Some stories have long expositions and precipitous falling action and minimal resolutions. Let the shape of the plot line show that relationship. "The Most Dangerous Game" by Richard Connell is an excellent choice for illustrating the types of conflict and an interesting plot structure. Ask students to label incidents in the rising action. This can be fun for them and you to see how consistently they can identify those plot events.

Lesson Three: Setting

The setting of a story is the time and place in which the action occurs. In a short story, the setting is particularly limited—sometimes just a single day or a few hours and in a single location. Here is a suggested schedule for engaging students in a review of what you have taught and an introduction to another basic element of story structure:

1. For ten minutes, review the elements of plot in the story students read. Ask them to work in pairs identifying those elements and the kind(s) of conflict.
2. Conduct a ten-to-fifteen-minute full-class discussion for students to share observations about the new story. This can be a think-pair-share format, or just turn and talk. It's important to build in time for students to talk using the terminology you are teaching.
3. For the remaining class period, guide the students through these new definitions:

   a. Setting in terms of time

   - Time of day: dawn, morning, afternoon, evening, night
   - Time of year: winter, spring, summer, fall
   - Time of life: childhood, teen years, adult, old age
   - Time in history: prehistoric, medieval, Elizabethan Age, future

   b. Setting in terms of place

   - Area of place: inside, outside, porch, roof, basement or cellar
   - Locale: city, country, mountains, sea, valley, forest
   - Continent: Africa, Asia, Europe, North or South America
   - Galaxy: Earth, another planet, another galaxy

4. Finally, assign a short story and ask students to pay close attention to ways the author establishes setting. Ask them to consider how the setting makes them feel or how setting creates a mood. Wait until the next period to remind them of the typical impact of daytime versus nighttime when good or bad things happen, rural versus urban places when the characters may be relaxed versus tense. Their responses to these locations may be inverted. Some students are more comfortable in the country and very tense in the city; some feel cloaked at night, exposed in the daytime.

If students are permitted to write in their textbooks, ask them to pencil rectangles around words or phrases that reveal setting and then write "T" in the margin for "time" and "P" in the margin for "place." If students are not permitted to write in their books, ask them to keep notes in their journal or use sticky notes. This active response to reading affirms for students what they are learning or reminds them about what they need to ask during the next class meeting.

Lesson Four: Characters—Act I

Fictional characters play roles and are developed to different degrees. The main character or protagonist usually attempts to solve the problem set forth in the exposition of the story. The antagonist is the opposing person (personal) or opposing force (impersonal). Authors create static or dynamic, flat or round characters, and reveal their personalities and motivations through direct and indirect means. Here is a schedule for the day's topic:

1. Have students work in pairs for ten to fifteen minutes on the homework, discussing ways the author used setting in the previous day's story. Note vivid language that creates mental pictures. You could ask students to choose colors to describe how they feel (the mood).
2. Conduct a P.I.E. class discussion, encouraging students to use literary vocabulary, backing up their views with specific passages from their texts.
3. Introduce the topic of characters. Show or reproduce the diagrams of conflicts.
4. List the main characters on the board and use them to review basic literary terms already introduced. Invite students to assign colors representing personalities of characters.

Be sure to remind students to write lecture-discussion notes in their journals to supplement the definitions, even hinting that a specific key concept might be on a quiz or test.

Some notes about characters:

- The *protagonist* is a human or other human-like character who struggles to overcome conflict. A story's suspense develops as a reader gets to know more about the protagonist and the ways this protagonist responds to obstacles.
- The *antagonist* is the opposing force (external forces include another character, a group, nature, technology, or even supernatural forces; internal forces refers to the conscience.)
- *Characterization* describes how authors reveal characters' personalities and motivations. Authors disclose such traits and motives directly or indirectly.

Here is a direct, expressed motive about the character "Claude": "Claude is a popular guy but is feared by most of the students in the school." If the author merely has other characters shrink away from and steer clear of Claude, then readers soon infer that characters in the story are afraid of Claude even though they are not told so directly through a statement by the author.

After introducing or reviewing facts about characters, ask your students to identify the kinds of characterization authors have used in stories read so far. Give your searchers time to find specific examples in the texts supporting their responses. Encourage students to talk among themselves as they seek out text clues. You could have students group to discuss chosen story, then share out. Once again, circulate among them, listening to their reasoning and gaining insight into their level of understanding. At the end of the session, summarize the terms and assign a new story.

Lesson Five: Characters—Act II

Character development is complicated and often needs an additional day of study. Explain how some characters develop and change during the story. One option is asking students why people do something right or wrong. The point is that people are complex; they act upon mixed motives. Real "characters" are not simple. In this regard, more complex fictional characters are like readers—and readers are like them. Show or reproduce the diagram on characters, and explain that for fictional purposes authors use a range of character types:

Dynamic and static characters: Usually, the protagonist is a dynamic character who changes and matures in the attempts to resolve the conflict. Most minor characters are static; they change very little or not at all.

Round and flat characters: Round characters learn more as the story progresses but might not change (like a balloon that grows larger as it is blown up but does not change its basic nature). Flat characters are usually

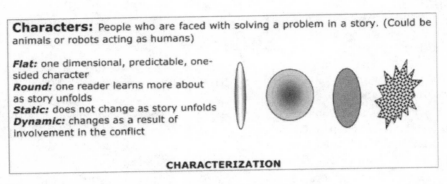

Characters: People who are faced with solving a problem in a story. (Could be animals or robots acting as humans)

Flat: one dimensional, predictable, one-sided character
Round: one reader learns more about as story unfolds
Static: does not change as story unfolds
Dynamic: changes as a result of involvement in the conflict

CHARACTERIZATION

Figure 3.2.   Writers develop characters in different ways

one-dimensional (like a paper doll), static, and often stereotypical (e.g., the pudgy best friend, the loyal sidekick, the shy and bespectacled nerd, the bully, and the fairy tale's evil stepmother). (See figure 3.2.)

Since this is the good stopping point for introducing new literary terms, review each one using all previous stories as examples. Then assign a more challenging story with more fully developed characters and a more complex plot. Edgar Allen Poe's short stories often fit this description but may be challenging for younger students or inexperienced English readers. Later lessons are designed to introduce additional literary devices.

Now that you know your students better, it may be an appropriate time to differentiate your instruction. Set up groups of four or five students based on common interests or current reading skills. Guided by what you have learned about your students so far, assign groups to read different stories from the anthology. If it suits your situation, two groups can read the same story. During the next class meetings those who have read the same stories could meet in small groups to discuss their findings using the literary vocabulary they are learning. Observe, listen, and take notes on who is confident using the new terms; who finds accurate examples to validate their claims about the story; who is encouraging and supportive; who sits and listens first, but responds with comments that show they know what is going on; and who hasn't a clue. All this anecdotal information can help you plan the next set of lessons tailored to meet the needs of your students.

WRITING ABOUT SHORT STORIES

A good time for a stress-free writing assessment is after this series of lessons, following up students' talking about the stories. Continue your focused observation as students work independently, then in small groups, and finally as a whole class. Here is an idea to help students summarize a story in three-to-five sentences using the basic journalistic questions: Who? What? When? Where? Why? How?

Model a way for students to glean specific information from a story:

- Who? List main characters—protagonist and antagonist(s)
- What? List seven to ten verbs that identify plot events. For example, choose a familiar story or movie. Ask the students to list verbs, using only the verbs for, say, "Goldilocks and the Three Bears": Goldilocks

1. walks.
2. sees.
3. peeks.
4. tastes.
5. sits.
6. sleeps.
7. awakens.
8. fears.
9. flees.

- When? When does the action occur—or from when to when?
- Where? Where does the majority of the action take place?
- Why? Why do the protagonist and antagonist act as they do—what drives or motivates them to act? Students may need help with vocabulary of motivation. You could offer ideas like fear, love, hunger, hate, power, greed, jealousy, and sense of adventure.
- How? How do the main characters accomplish their deeds—physically, mentally, both?

After you introduce students to the basic reportorial story categories, use the fairy tale or movie plot to write a three-to-five-sentence summary with the students so they get the idea.

After group brainstorming, permit students to work independently for ten minutes or so to write their own summaries. If time permits, conclude the period by having one student from each group read his or her summary aloud while the rest of the class decides whether each reader has included all six requirements. What's missing? Who can add the missing information?

Be ready to assemble students into brainstorming groups to gather facts, in eight to ten minutes, about one of the stories they have just read. Two groups can work on the same story, as needed. Tell them they will report their findings to the rest of the class. When someone from each group reports, point out that groups sometimes identify different Ws or Hs in their responses. Be open with students about the fact that different interpretations can both be correct

Students make good teachers

because stories and their characters are often complex—unlike simplistic TV commercials or cartoons with stereotypical characters.

This reportorial activity provides a good appraisal of readiness for a test or quiz on literary terms and story elements. If students are ready, give them a test or quiz in a day or so. If not, take a couple of days to work with simpler stories and to practice identifying elements and using text evidence to support opinions and observations. See your own anthology resources or check online for a sample quiz on these typical terms. Skills developed here, writing summaries about short stories, will come in handy when you teach students how to conduct research and want them to write summaries of their findings.

SUMMARIZING TEXT AS A POEM

Sometimes inviting students to summarize a fictional text as a narrative poem is an engaging and effective way to conduct a formative assessment of their reading, of poetry writing, and of teamwork. Middle School teacher Audrey Spica found this quick way to assess just before Christmas school break and after students had studied the classic novel *A Christmas Carol* by Charles Dickens. She had her seventh graders work in quintets; this is an unedited example of five students collaborating to write a character poem about Ebenezer Scrooge:

A Christmas Carol Poem

Stanza 1 - Sarah

There's Ebenezer Scrooge with his curmudgeon ways
And Bob Cratchit who works all his tiring days
There's Fred, Scrooge's Nephew, who beckons every call
And Tiny Tim, Bob's son, who blesses us all
It's a cold day in England, winter all around
Christmas time fills the place with jolly sounds

Stanza 2 - Erika

Scrooge never got a wife
He had a pretty sad life.
His love for money, overruled his love
He sure wasn't, a peaceful, loving dove.
Everyone knew that Scrooge didn't have a great soul
For holiday's he only gets coal.
Scrooge has really, never cared about anyone
Or ever having just a little fun.

Stanza 3 - Jaevyn

A cold breeze swept through
The ghost knew
For sat idly by
Was a sign that scrooge had died
Shivers down his spine
As dearest death was defined
Now a witness to death, he stood illy
Will he, will he, will he die?
Not a soul in sight?
Spoken poorly of?
If only he'd shown more love . . .

Stanza 4 - Sarah

Scrooge looms the streets, a smile on his face
He hops with joy all throughout the place
Spreading cheer around the town
With Scrooge, no one could ever frown
Fun at Fred's Party, making new friends
Scrooge wished that this bliss would never end

Stanza 5 - Cadence

Scrooge once was a man
Who destroyed others plans
But now he has changed
His life rearranged
He has seen his own grave
Now changing his ways is his only crave
Now making people happy was his thing
Now joy around the town is what he'd bring

DIGITIZING STUDENT OBSERVATIONS

What fun! Collaborate, review, produce, reinforce, decorate, learn, and teach with online CLOUD generators. For a whole class, in small groups or as individuals, you can invite students to use online generators to create artwork reflecting responses to reading. Then post results around the classroom or on class website. If space is limited let the class decide which one(s) to post, or post them one per day or week.

Ask students to write a paragraph describing a character, summarizing events in a scene, discussing the theme of a novel or play, highlighting main ideas in an essay, or critiquing a movie, and then make a CLOUD using a website like tagxedo.com or wordclouds.com. Or . . . you could make a class cloud by having students write one of the following:

- Ten words describing one of the main characters
- One sentence summarizing a recently read scene from the literary work
- One sentence stating in their own words one of the main ideas in the story
- One sentence critiquing the literary work

Then in groups of five, invite students to post their group's lists (keep duplicate words so that each cloud represents all fifty words), or all the sentences into one of the cloud text screens, then create and print their group cloud. If reviewing a longer work or play, divide the book into chapters or sections, or into scenes or acts for a play, and let students sign up for their preferred scene. Remember, the more times a single word appears in the text, the more prominently it will appear in the cloud. That's the point.

Next, create a class collage of all the group clouds. This should make for an interesting visual summary of what students are thinking, observing, and concluding. When these word clouds are posted, recurrent words and phrases will highlight and thus reinforce key observations.

INTRODUCING OR REVIEWING TEXT STRUCTURES

One essential skill in active reading is recognizing how subparts of a larger text relate to one another. These text structures, sometimes called "rhetorical structures," include descriptive, sequential, enumerative, cause-effect, problem/solution, and compare/contrast relationships within a text. Depending on where students went to school before becoming your students, they may or may not be familiar with text structures or have not used the terms describing the ways texts, especially nonfiction, may be organized. Do not be surprised if you find it necessary to introduce or reteach this language.

Your students may recognize some text features in expository nonfiction works and may need to be reminded of ways text features work in fiction. In this case, they are paying attention to chapter titles, images that may be added to certain pages, diagrams, maps, charts, or unexpected spacing that sometimes appear in fiction.

Chapter titles are often signals of what follows. Authors of modern fiction sometimes choose to write from multiple points of view and the only clue to these changes may be an extra space between paragraphs or a flourish or line to indicate this shift in perspective. Students may be confused if they miss these subtle cues. If necessary, go online and locate a site that concisely teaches the language. There are some clever short videos to introduce or review this approach to reading texts. More ideas will arise as you read chapter 4 on compelling writing.

APPLYING NEWLY LEARNED SKILLS—BOOK REPORT #1

The end of the first quarter is a great opportunity to have students independently apply what they are learning about the elements of fiction, but in a text, they are reading individually. If it is not realistic to expect your students to complete a book outside of class, plan ahead to allot twenty to twenty-five minutes daily for the next couple of weeks for students to read in class. To make efficient use of the full-period time, set up a schedule so that all students study/practice grammar or focused writing instruction for about half the period. Chapter 8 has ideas for teaching grammar, directly or indirectly, as part of your writing instruction. You can make that determination based on the grade and skill level of the students as revealed in writing you have already seen in earlier assignments.

Informal speaking activities conducted early in the semester can help students develop confidence for longer speeches in class. You can see how they are progressing, meeting curriculum standards that ask students to

demonstrate how well they can give oral presentations that are uncompli-
cated, even for students for whom English is not their first language. See
chapter 7 for guidelines for teaching oral communications more specifically.

Here are some ideas to consider for book reports. (Note that Option
A adapts very well for a book report on biographical texts.)

Making Connections in Three Parts

Step 1—Select and read a novel.
Step 2—Create a diagram of the plot.
Step 3—Write a summary of your novel.
Step 4—Decide Option A or Option B and write a meaty P.I.E. paragraph
response.
Step 5—Present your report with your classmates on the due date
_____.

Part I

1. Use one side of a 12 × 9" sheet of construction paper or one digital slide.
2. Draw a plot line that shows how the events in your story progressed. If you
   have a longer exposition than resolution, have the length of lines reflect
   that. If you have a shorter rising action than falling action, let your plot
   line show that.
3. Show the following in words and drawings, computer graphics, or magazine cutouts.

- Main characters
- Setting
- Conflict
- Complications/obstacles in rising action
- Climax
- Falling action/denouement
- Resolution

Part II

Reverse side of the same construction paper or digital slide(s)—Word-
process your paragraph, print it, and then glue it on the paper, OR copy
and paste to slide(s) using twenty-four point font and seven to ten words
per slide.

Write a half-page summary of your book that includes the title, author,
main characters, and the characterization author uses; the setting—both time
and place; the conflict—specify kind(s); and the point of view. *Use literary*

terms we've been learning. Paste on the left side of the back page or on digital slides using an easy-to-read font.

Part III

Write a half-page paragraph response to Option A or Option B. Decide which questions best fit your book. (Consider them all, then write about three or four.) Organize your responses so that your paragraph flows smoothly from one idea to the next. Word-process your paragraph, print out, and then glue on to reverse side of poster. Paste on the right side of the back page or on a separate digital slide. For this part, paste the whole paragraph on one slide.

Option A—My Response to This Book

First, answer these questions about your book; then decide which are more significant to you and then pull your responses together into a unified paragraph.

For example: Qualities of character, connection to character, opinions expressed, expectations, and so on.

1. What did you like best about the person you read about? Why?
2. What did you like least about the person you read about? Why?
3. Does this person remind you of yourself? Explain your answer.
4. What is the most difficult moment for this person? What does he or she learn from it?
5. What is the best moment for this person? What does he or she learn from it?
6. Which qualities of this person would you want to develop within yourself?
7. Why would you like to develop these qualities?
8. Do any of the ideas, incidents, or actions in this book remind you of your own life, or something that has happened to you?
9. Do you feel that there is an opinion expressed by the author in this book? What is it? Why do you think this is an opinion? Do you agree with the opinion? Why or why not?
10. From what point of view is the book written? How would the book be different if it were written from a different point of view? Which one?
11. When you picked the book, what kind did you think it would be? Why? Was it what you thought it would be? If not, did you like it anyway?

Option B—This Book Made Me . . .

Complete each of these eight ideas with specific information from the book you read.

This book made me

- wish that . . .
- realize that . . .
- decide that . . .
- wonder about . . .
- see that . . .
- believe that . . .
- feel that . . .
- and hope that . . .

Decide which ideas are more significant to you, then write a unified paragraph that pulls them together. Remember to write a P.I.E. paragraph: Make point; illustrate point with details from your book; explain to show connection between illustration and point.

CONCLUSION

The key to introducing narrative theory in middle school language arts and adults new to college is to use examples and illustrations from stories that engage students; keep them reading, viewing, listening, and sharing stories and other texts. Use stories from the class text along with downloadable media files, especially short video clips.

The short-term goal is to have a common word base and academic concepts of the grammar of fiction, and a concrete understanding of these elements of literature. The longer-term goal is to prepare your students with knowledge and skills that can serve them well when they reach high school, perhaps go on to college, take future courses, and eventually participate in neighborhood book-discussion groups they may join as adults. Right?

NOTE

1. Sybylla Y. Hendrix, "Why Our Students Study Literature," Gustavus Adolphus College, 2012. http://gustavus.edu/academics/english/whystudyliterature.php (accessed April 3, 2012).

Chapter 4

Compelling Writing: Informational to Persuasive

People are usually more convinced by reasons they discovered themselves than by those found out by others.[1]

—Blaise Pascal

Writing is a personal way to express oneself. While purpose determines the mode one uses, the structure, length, style, and order one writes remain the choice of the author. This fact creates a dilemma for teachers charged with teaching students specific ways to write and obligated to test students on their ability to write in different modes. Unless teachers plan carefully, this predicament could reduce the time they allot for students to choose the most effective ways of communicating to achieve their personal purposes. This chapter describes ways to manage this quandary with suggestions for teaching the basics, and freeing students to write for real purposes.

In the classroom, it sometimes is easy to lose sight of the ultimate goal of education—to help students acquire knowledge and develop the range of skills needed to live self-sufficient, productive lives in a pluralistic society. However, as teachers work backward, knowing the goal and designing lessons to help reach that goal, they learn to stay on track without becoming rigidly shortsighted.

So what does this have to do with teaching students how to write? It means remembering that our classroom is a training ground where we, as coaches, introduce new information, demonstrate skills, and then schedule opportunities for students to learn and practice writing, but ultimately, when the game begins, trust even young adolescents to choose what works in the heat of the game—when they want to write to express themselves.

Standards for writing used in your school likely require teachers to present a range of proven strategies for prewriting, revising, editing, and publishing.

Successful educators somehow learn to do this without insisting that every student execute each step in the same way for every assignment. You know from your own schooling, college training, and work in the classroom that there probably are as many different configurations for prewriting, drafting, and revising as years you have been on this earth! None works well for every writer every time. Ask the zillion published authors out there. So, considering this reality, how does one teach?

Make plans guided by curriculum standards and remain flexible. This chapter is designed to help you navigate this part of your trip. No need to worry. You can steer through the tricky waters without fearing Scylla and Charybdis, those rocks and whirlpools that could distract you from teaching writing effectively.

LEARNING FROM A STUDENT—A PERSONAL STORY

After weeks of instruction, I just knew my young writers were ready to move on to the next step: applying what they'd learned about the writing process in an on-demand timed setting. I'd taught them well. They'd responded enthusiastically. Now, I thought, is their time to shine and my time to gloat? Not.

They arrived to see an engaging prompt on the board and the starting and stop times written prominently as a reminder to pace themselves. It was time to commence the show. Students pulled out pens, sheets of lined loose-leaf paper, and a piece of scratch paper on which to create their prewrites. No more questions? They got started. I strolled around the room, observing their writing, nodding as I noticed nearly every option for prewriting appear among the papers I could see. Good!

Then, I spotted one girl across the room gazing off into space. "Hmmm. Why isn't she writing?" Carefully, so as not to alarm anyone, I quickly made my way over to her desk and peered around her shoulder, glaring in disbelief. Her paper was blank, nothing there, no list, no diagram, no drawing, nothing after nearly fifteen minutes into the period! How was she going to finish in time? I leaned down and whispered, "What's the hold-up? When are you going to get started?"

She whispered back, "I'm thinking."

A little louder, but still keeping my voice low, I asked, "Can't you see the clock?"

"Yeah, I see it. I'm OK. I'm thinking." "When are you going to start writing? "When I can see my paper."

"See your paper?" I quietly yelled. She glowered, letting me know she had things under control and wouldn't I just trust her and shut up and let her

finish, for crying out loud, didn't I see the clock? I got the message, shrugged my shoulders, pursed my lips, and let it go, dooming her to her fate. She was going to be a disappointment. I certainly didn't look forward to reading a paper not written the way I'd spent so much time teaching.

As you probably surmised, this student's paper was one of the better ones in the bunch. I was surprised, yes, and just a little disenchanted. I apparently hadn't been the one to teach her how to write so well in a timed setting. *Who had?*

Thankfully, the young lady was easy going; she didn't appear the least bit concerned when I invited her in to talk about the paper. I asked how she organized her thoughts if she wasn't using any of the prewriting strategies I'd demonstrated so assiduously and seen her practice so enthusiastically. She acknowledged that she'd done all the exercises because they were fun, but they didn't really work that well for her. *Is that so!*

She explained that she produced better writing when she brainstormed, organized, and reorganized her thoughts in her head. She even visualized what her paper would look like. Then she just wrote what she saw. "Well! That's just great," I thought. "How am I going to grade a student's prewrite if I can't see it. Should I insist she do things the way I taught her, just so I'd have something to grade? Even if what she produces is good without them?" *Thanks a lot for this quandary!*

The young lady left. Trying to sort out my thoughts, I recalled research about multiple intelligences. Students process information in different ways

Students resort to strategies that work best for them

and here was concrete evidence. While this student did not fall into the typical alternative categories that show up on the Howard Gardner charts—auditory, kinesthetic, musical, and the like—hers was a distinctively different style from those I had encountered before. The diverse strategies presented by the teacher leaders I had heard at professional conferences, what I learned from experience and reading, is apparently not all there is to writing. I'd have to make some adjustments.

After that incident, I recognized the need for even more flexibility and differentiation in options offered for students to show what they know. Planning lessons, I became more conscientious about what I have to assess. Then during instruction, I strived to articulate what I need to measure about students' learning, confirming their level of understanding and degree of skill development. More and more often, I offer alternative assessments and let students choose ways they can best show what they know. I urge you to do the same.

WRITING RIGHT: JUST THE RIGHT MODE FOR THE OCCASION

The five-paragraph essay may be one of many structures you are expected to teach. It is a formula designed to encourage students to flesh out their writing by developing their position statements into meaty paragraphs. However, this prescribed mold does not work well for some students, and it is seldom seen in professional publications. So rather than adhere strictly to a formula that can stifle writing, teach it as an option, but do not require every student to write this way for every essay assigned.

Alternatively, teach students the parts of an essay: introduction, body, and conclusion, as well as the *function* of each part. For some new writers, three paragraphs are sufficient for what they have to say and the way they can say it best. For others, four will suffice; other may need six or more paragraphs. In other words, remain flexible about the number of paragraphs, words, and pages you expect. Insist, instead, that the final essay include the necessary parts.

Acting Out an Essay

How about a little kinesthetic activity to help students understand the structure of an essay? You could invite small groups of seven to ten students to demonstrate an essay that has three parts. Jock Mackenzie, author of *Essay Writing: Teaching the Basics from the Ground Up*, recommends inviting students to organize themselves into an essay with at least three groups, representing the introduction, the body, and the conclusion. This may take a little time, so help pace the steps using your timer.

For the first step, set your timer for five to seven minutes, depending on the number of students and classroom space. Then step aside, listen, and watch how students decide who should stand, where, and why. When the timer rings, ask the students to freeze and look around. You could ask those in the introduction section to raise their hands; those in the section(s) for body paragraph(s) to raise their hands, and then those in the conclusion section to do the same.

What are you looking to see? Proportion. Are there fewer students in the introduction and conclusion sections? Direct the three groups to assemble in separate corners of the room to establish a group gesture or body pose that would indicate the function of their part of the essay. Again, set the time for five to seven minutes; step aside, observe and listen to what they do and say.

For example, the introduction group may arrange themselves into a triangle with each member gesturing forward with their pointer finger to indicate the introduction shows the way the essay will go. One person may decide to demonstrate the thesis statement. The body group may arrange themselves into two or more smaller groups to indicate multiple paragraphs or sections. Each subgroup may have one student representing the topic sentence in some way. The conclusion group may stand and gesture "time-out" to indicate that the essay is coming to an end. This group may arrange itself in a triangle and point thumbs over shoulders to indicate that the conclusion may look back to point to what has already been developed in the body.

Finally, ask students to demonstrate the need for transitions between sections and sentences by reaching out and linking pinky fingers. Yes, they will giggle, but that's typical. Then call a freeze and pause for silence. If you have a digital camera or cell phone, snap a photo before directing students to return to their seats. Close with a debriefing session reflecting on the choices they made and how their final tableau demonstrated the structure of an essay. In the lessons to come, remind them of this exercise and maybe point to the photo of them that you post on the bulletin board or upload into a slide you can project during class.

Choosing Topics for Writing

An effective way to get to know travelers on a trip through the school year is to invite them to talk about themselves. This also is an efficient way to obtain baseline writing from your students of any age. Talking and writing about themselves removes the additional burden of showing what they know about an assigned topic, piece of fiction or nonfiction writing they have read. Your student writers can pay attention to organization, sentence structure, and choice of language. You can wait until later in the year to measure how well they can pull in evidence from literary or informational texts to support their analysis, reflection, and research.

Yes, some students are reluctant to write about personal matters in an unfamiliar or uncomfortable setting. It may take weeks before your class-room environment feels safe. So consider assignments in which students can fictionalize details if they wish. One such assignment that can work asks students to consider their futures and the value of education and career planning. It is writing a human-interest story—about themselves. While you know that choices they make reveal the writer, the students experience the detachment that makes them feel more secure.

Consider the assignment given next. It combines the two—opportunity to talk about themselves and to fictionalize a future event. It even has an option for conducting informal research as students consider the qualifications for certain awards. Preparing for this writing, students can learn the criteria for various awards and come to an understanding that awards are given for out-standing performance, contributions, and excellence in a career: community service, philanthropy, science, the arts, sports, and other areas. Your students may choose well-known Nobel Prize awards in the various categories; the Oscar, Grammy, Tony, and other awards for the arts; Halls of Fame for vari-ous sports: Cy Young Award, MVP awards; rodeo, fishing, ballroom dancing; Miss America or Mr. Universe; or those lesser known but coveted awards given in your hometown or state.

With minor editing, these articles will make fine additions to your class bulletin board, class website, inserts for letters to families, or saved and handed back at the end of school year journey.

Human Interest Story

With what prestigious award will you be honored in twenty-five years?

> Paragraph 1: Who, what, when, where, why, and how about award ceremony
>
> Paragraph 2: Education and career of winner (you in twenty-five years)
>
> Paragraph 3: Others who have won the honor in the past
>
> Paragraph 4: Ways this year's winner (you) compares to former winners
>
> Paragraph 5: When and where award ceremony takes place next year

After revising and editing your article, add a recent photo of yourself. Refer to General Grading Guidelines to see how this will be evaluated.

DISCOVERING PURPOSES AND
ORGANIZATION PATTERNS

You have required curriculum to follow, right? As general policy, introducing or reviewing specific modes of writing, letting students write about themselves, and giving students choices all sound good, but you still may wonder where to start. Why not at the beginning?

Let your current students discover or be reminded about the elements found in different modes of writing. You may begin with brainstorming, asking students to list a range of reasons people would want to write in the first place. The list should include such purposes as

- to inform,
- to explain,
- to report,
- to argue,
- to persuade,
- to entertain, and more.

Use the students' words first to validate their contribution. You then can move along and add the more formal terms. It will be important, ultimately, for students to know the academic vocabulary leading to success in other educational settings, like those end-of-the-year exams, many schools administer on which these terms may appear.

Setting Up the Discovery Expedition

Gather age-appropriate samples or mentor texts of different types of writing in your textbook and online. Look for culturally responsive writing on topics that interest your students and that introduce topics you may be teaching later in the school year. No need to leave out essays that are humorous. They sometimes are more accessible and memorable.

Organize the samples and subtly color code similar kinds of writing with a rainbow color to match the groups: red, green, blue, purple, yellow, and orange. Resist the temptation to rush the process by giving students clues ahead of time. Let them discover by talking with partners or in small groups.

Create slides with the step-by-step instructions so that students not paying close attention can glance up, confirm they heard you right, and get back to work. Usually, one slide per step will suffice. You can advance the slides as the class completes each step. Have slides prepared with five or six COLOR GROUPS with names listed next to letters A–F. These slides serve as guides for grouping and regrouping later. Decide, based on your understanding of the class, whether you need to set up these groups or whether students can do this voluntarily. Have your timer ready.

- Start with a version of the think, pair, share option. First, let students read the sample on their own.
- Set the timer for about three minutes for each step. It is okay if students do not finish reading the entire essay each time. They are doing preliminary investigation. You can project the entire list of kinds based on list given earlier.
- Hand out colored pencils and ask students to read silently the first sample and mark anything that clues them to the *kind of essay* they have.
- Exchange pencils for a new color. Read the sample again, this time marking what they recognize in terms of *text structure and organization*.
- Exchange pencils once more, getting a third color. This time, read and mark *beginning*, *middle*, and *end* of the sample essay. Students may need four minutes this time.

  - A triangle pointing down next to the beginning section.
  - A rectangle where the middle or body begins.
  - A triangle pointing up to mark the start of the ending section.

- Finally, ask students to write what they think is the purpose of their sample essay: to inform, explain, compare, argue, persuade, entertain, or whatever.

If your students are using tablets or computers, consider having students use a different color highlighting for each step and inserting comments identifying the part of the essay.

During this initial ten to twelve minutes when students are working independently, remember to circulate among them paying attention to which students get started quickly. Who seems to be puzzled and needs you to re-explain what they should be doing? Your physical proximity helps these student investigators stay focused and ask questions without attracting embarrassing peer attention. This would be a good time to write some anecdotal notes about what you observe. Remember to advance your slides showing the prompt for each reading.

Grouping Homogenously and Heterogeneously

- After ten minutes or so working independently, change to the slide showing the color and have them gather into COLOR teams, based on your color code on their papers, and let them work together for twelve to fifteen minutes.

Circulate, observe, and plan next steps

- Now students in color-team groups look carefully at their samples and discuss what they have marked as they paid attention to the features, marking identifying content and structure based on their observations and how they labeled their writing sample.
- Ask the student sleuths to list characteristics of the writing they put into the categories.
- Urge groups to try reaching consensus about the kind of essays they have, but it is not essential. The discussion is what is important during this discovery expedition.
- Set your timer to remind you to stop and move them into their heterogeneous, rainbow teams.
- Show slides with color groups and names of students in each one. These rainbow group members identified as A, B, C, D, E, and F should now reorganize in letter groups (next to their names on the slides) so that groups now include all five or six colors. Set the timer again for twelve to fifteen minutes for this next step.

During these group meetings, each color-group representative should explain to the others how their members labeled their sample(s) and what organization and text-structure clues helped them decide the purpose of their sample essay. As before, listening and observing can help you decide what they already know and what still needs clarification. Thankfully, students often are good teachers and save your valuable time by explaining the key points in ways their peers understand.

Finally, call the class together to merge their findings and reflect on what they have discovered. How consistent are the findings? What characteristics do students notice in different samples?

Taking Time for Discovery

These discovery expeditions may take two or three days. No need to rush. If it makes sense to send the samples home for homework review, do so. Then, during the next class, reassemble the adventurers into rainbow groupings when the class meeting begins. If this kind of homework is unrealistic, begin the next class in the single-color groups to review what they discovered. After ten minutes or so, move the students into the rainbow groups.

After the independent, homogeneous, then heterogeneous looks at the samples, the students are likely to have detected some of the patterns of organizing that you taught them to watch for when they are reading to learn.

- Description
- Sequential Order
- Problem-Solution
- Compare/Contrast
- Cause/Effect
- Directions

You can first try to keep it simple but be prepared for students to notice that writers may use one or more of these structures to fulfill any of the purposes for writing: to inform, to argue, to persuade, or to entertain. So you really are asking students to try to identify the purpose for the writing, to notice the use of text structures as well as the patterns of organization.

It also is likely they may find it difficult to distinguish between the samples you may have included that illustrate argument and those that exemplify persuasion. You may have to point out, after such a discussion, that argumentation simply presents opposing views and maybe even reasons for believing one side or the other, while persuasion usually includes a call for action, a plea to change one's belief or behavior.

TEACHING IS MORE THAN TELLING

Yes, this kind of teaching will take more time than giving a lecture, showing slides with definitions, or even labeling writing samples and highlighting the different features; in that case, *you* will have done the thinking. More effective teaching and long-term retention occur when students seek out and find answers for themselves. What students discover for themselves, they remember.

This may mean less reteaching on your part, but you still will find it useful to plan a variety of alternative methods of lesson delivery until the majority of the students can demonstrate they have learned. Effective teachers teach spirally, drawing earlier lessons into current ones so students hear, see, and do enough to develop proficiency. Because the lessons will look different, the students are less likely to think you are merely being repetitive.

Learning to Use Text Structure

If during these exploratory activities, it is clear your students are not yet confident talking about text structures and these terms are not defined or explained in your textbook, no need to worry. Several websites include definitions and mini-lessons to help you get started. Most suggest that teachers

- introduce the idea that expository texts have a text structure.
- introduce common text structures.
- show examples of paragraphs that correspond to each text structure.
- examine topic sentences with signal words that clue the reader to a specific structure.
- model the writing of a paragraph that uses a specific structure.
- have students experiment with writing paragraphs that follow a structure.

Even with increased implementation of teaching strategies that appeal to multiple intelligences, consider building in reteaching, but with a twist. Plan multisensory lessons that require students to use physical as well as mental muscles. Remember the earlier activity that asked for students to "Act Out an Essay." These kinds of lessons include something for students to see, hear, and do. Note recommendations for kinesthetic presentations as you continue reading this book.

Will you have to remind students of what they have seen, heard, and done? Of course. You very well may have some of these same students in later grades and shake your head that they may have forgotten so much of what you thought you had taught so well. That probably is the main reason students have English classes nearly every school year—not just because language forms the basis for learning in most content areas but also because students forget or see no immediate use for what they are taught. If they do not use it, they lose it. Teachers continue to provide multiple opportunities for students to exercise their skills, so their thinking muscles will not atrophy, thus making it difficult to use these muscles when they need them.

Writing to Explore, Explain, and Expand Thinking

You may be teaching courses other than English or may be on teams with teachers in other content areas. Share with them the value of using ungraded writing assignment as ways for students to explore, explain, and expand their thinking about the topic and ways they are learning. Reading these short writings provides insight for both students and teachers and will inform your teaching and their studying.

Cassidy Earle, a math teacher of sixth-grade students, frequently assigns writing as informal formative assessments. In them, students reveal both comprehension and misunderstandings about their learning more concretely than in class discussions or on quizzes. She sometimes asks how they studied, what they learned, how they felt about their learning, how would they rationalize their answers, and other questions that explore practical applications for math concepts. One student wrote, "If you are building a wheel chair ramp, you have to know about right angles to not make it too steep. But you can't make it too steep that it doesn't reach the destination."

While you may smile at the wording of the response, it is clear that this student understands a real-world application of geometry concepts related to angles. Use writing for these purposes and share the strategy with teachers with whom you work. They will be glad to know that to be useful, all writing does not have to be graded for grammatical correctness.

Carefully build a firm foundation

BUILDING THE FOUNDATION FOR
CONVINCING ARGUMENTATIVE ESSAYS

An effective way to teach students to write argumentative essays is to take time to build on skills they already have learned. Most middle school students have been writing reports since third grade. It makes sense, then, to embark on this part of the trip that includes a direct writing instruction unit by having your students practice writing to inform because that simply requires that students gather, organize, and present facts in much the same way as those elementary school science reports.

So begin there. "What," you could ask them, "are some of the reasons a person would want to write an informative essay?" Their answers are likely to include such things as to report, to explain, to describe, and to just share their feelings. You probably will have taught text structures already as they relate to readings, and earlier in their expedition with essays. Now is the time to have students demonstrate what they understand about text structures by employing those devices in their own writing. Post on your website, include on printed assignments, and display on your word wall some of the signal words used in published informative writing and probably listed in the textbook you are using.

You could have students begin reporting or explaining about something they already know. Their topics could come from literature, real life, or lessons students are learning in other content areas. In fact, inviting them to write about what they are learning in science, social studies, art, and music is an excellent way to reinforce what your students are learning elsewhere and to validate the work of colleagues in other departments. Varied topics make for more interesting, even informative, reading for you, too.

Consider inviting your companions on the road to write about a historical event; explain how to accomplish a task—build something, cook, sail, fish, rope a steer, ride a horse, pop an "Ollie" in their skateboard, or strategize in a board or computer game. To reduce student temptation to copy from published work, begin the drafting in class. If students then decide to do research before the final draft is due, remind them to cite their sources. As always on a multi-draft assignment, students should date, keep, and turn in all drafts, earliest on the bottom; latest on the top. If they are working online, date and save all drafts so they and you can see how their writing evolves.

TAKING LOGICAL STEPS
TO OTHER KINDS OF WRITING

The next logical step—move on to writing compare/contrast essays for which students gather, organize, and write about two different people, places, things, events, or ideas. To keep this concrete, again invite students to consider something they already know about. You could have them compare/contrast short stories they have read for your class and one they read on their own; movies or television programs on the same topic that students have viewed; kinds of music; food; different computer games; clothes; animals; or cars, bicycles, boats, fishing rods, or saddles.

Show your budding writers two basic ways of organizing compare/contrast essays and invite them to choose the pattern that works better for them. They could write the body of their paragraphs in blocks or strips.

- Blocks

    - Introduce the features to be considered
    - All comparisons or ways alike
    - All contrasts or ways different

- Strips

    - Feature or comparison 1—A and B together
    - Feature or comparison 2—A and B together
    - Feature or comparison 3—A and B together

Their task is to decide what features or elements to compare or contrast. A Venn diagram is an effective graphic organizer for brainstorming and arranging the facts and explanations about how the two subjects of the essay are alike or different.

For example, students may look at two stories and compare different ways the authors employ literary devices: What point of view? What dominant method of characterization? Are there flashbacks? Use of dialogue? Or, keeping it personal, they may compare/contrast themselves and the main character in a biographical work they are assigned to read. See this book companion website for a list of recommended autobiographies, biographies, and memoirs you may assign your students during the second quarter, and then use as the basis for this and other writing.

For a basic compare/contrast essay, the students are simply reporting, but you may ask them to add an element of evaluation and write about which author each student thinks uses the literary or rhetorical elements more effectively; which product, song, or sport is better in some defined way; or why fishing with one kind of rod is safer than another. Then the writers will be moving into argumentation, making a case for one story, product, or the other. While it is okay to use "I think" and "I believe" in earlier drafts, ask the students to avoid saying "I think" in the final draft. Just state their observations and let those statements stand firmly based on the reasons the students give for taking those positions on the topic, thus encouraging students to develop confidence in their supported assertions.

WRITING THAT SHOWS AND TELLS

One of the ways to help students expand their writing without simply blowing it up with frivolous air is to have them show and not just tell what they think or believe about their topic. Naturally confident writers may resist at first when they are asked to write about a topic you have chosen. When reminded that whatever they write reflects their thinking, students usually become more conscientious. This is another time to remind them about the "I" in P.I.E. writing. The P is telling the reader the writer's position: what he or she thinks or believes. The "I" brings in illustrations—examples, anecdotes, and facts—that help the reader see what the writer means. The "E" explains with reasons how and why the illustrations show or prove the writer's point.

Sample Template: (Note transition words in Italics.)

State your POSITION (or opinion on the topic). *For example,* (ILLUSTRATE with quotations, facts, or examples from literature or from life). *This shows* (In two or three sentences EXPLAIN or expand the link between the illustration and the point.)

- *Furthermore,* (another ILLUSTRATION).
- *This shows* . . . (In two or three sentences EXPLAIN).
- *Moreover,* (another ILLUSTRATION).

One can see how (In two or three sentences EXPLAIN or SUMMARIZE).

SAMPLE P.I.E. PARAGRAPH

Learning to write is an important skill for anyone to develop whether a teenager or a grownup. For example, teachers learn what students understand from what they write. This shows that young people who want to get good grades in school will have to write well enough to show what they know. Furthermore, people use writing to help take care of problems in their personal and professional lives. Some adults write letters to apply for a job; others write letters to explain why they are behind on their payments. Sometimes a person loses his job and just can't keep up those payments. A well-written letter may be just what is needed to get an extension, so they can pay the bills later without penalty. One can see that both young and older people have good reasons to be able to express themselves clearly in writing.

Some students respond well to this approach to developing paragraphs when you offer a template or suggest a required number of sentences for each paragraph. In the early weeks of the school year with inexperienced writers or those new to writing in English, you could require nine-sentence paragraphs; then raise the number up to eleven or thirteen. Each sentence in the draft should fulfill one of the P.I.E. structure functions. Also remind the students to add transition words and phrases that show relationships among sentences. By the final draft, the number of sentences may well be fewer or more, and some transitions may be deleted without losing the flow of ideas; requiring specific components in early drafts helps students organize and expand their writing in a meaningful way.

CONNECTING WRITING TO CURRENT EVENTS

To keep the learning relevant, you could ask students to bring in samples from their reading that exemplify the kind of writing you are teaching. To help focus their searches, direct students to bring in articles that would interest a character or person in a story, book, or essay the class has studied together.

Several students come from homes where magazines and newspapers are regularly read. Direct the rest to school or neighborhood libraries where they can find samples in magazines and newspapers to which most libraries subscribe. You could offer students minimum credit for bringing in articles, but no need to penalize anyone who does not. You know your school community and can choose assignments that affirm the households from which your students come and utilize resources readily available to them. Remember the magazines in your closet?

If you know all class members do not have comparable access to resources, you could schedule a library visit, or consider making this a triad or small group project. In that case, one student can bring in the article(s); another mount them on white sheet(s) of paper and mark the parts, and another can speak for the group, describing the article(s)' contents, kind(s) of writing, and special features the group has noticed. In this situation, the value is in the students talking, making decisions about how to present what they are learning about published writing.

A benefit of assigning students to bring in samples is the insight you gain into what interests them. You can use that knowledge to design subsequent assignments. Depending on your school community, students may bring in articles from *ESPN* or *Sports Illustrated*, *People* or *Time*, and *Car and Driver* or *Teen Vogue* magazines. Some of your techy teens may regularly read zines online and print something from one of those sites. Remind those students that to earn the bonus points, they must include the citation that includes the website name, title, authors, URL address, and date they access the article. Those who bring in printed articles should label them with source and date.

It is prudent to check articles brought in to assure they are appropriate for in-class discussion. Your students may not yet know exactly what is off-limits in the classroom. Conduct an inspection subtly by having students bring in articles at least a day before you plan to have them meet in triads to talk about them. Just discretely remove questionable articles and offer that group a magazine from which to choose another. No need to create a scene. Some students have different sets of standards and, no matter how they shock you, you can help them develop discernment without embarrassing them.

What makes this kind of student-generated assignment so rich is that students tend to read more when they can choose what to contribute. Students usually want to make sure they understand the selection, just in case you ask them to talk about it! Some may want to impress you and their peers and bring in articles from *Business Week* or *Atlantic Monthly* that they or their parents regularly read. Even though this is middle school or remedial community college course, some of the students truly may be interested in articles from what generally are considered sophisticated journals. So act as though you expected nothing less.

DECIDING HOW LONG

So far, in these writing assignments, students are not being required to argue a position to bring about a change in belief or behavior. They have been gathering facts and writing about them in some logically organized fashion. Whatever the assignments, they probably have begun to ask, "How long should this be?" You may be tempted to say, "Long enough to get the job done," which is a good answer, but not very helpful to young or inexperienced writers. Instead, you could tell them that to be complete, an essay, like a good story, should have at least three parts: a recognizable beginning, middle, and ending. For an essay, the names of these parts are introduction, body, and conclusion.

Now is a good time to teach or review with your curious writers the function of each of these parts of an essay. Yes,—even if you have bright, know-it-all eighth or ninth graders, or even first-year community college students, who have been writing very well all through school—you should go over these functions in as much in depth as needed with your current students, then hold them accountable

- for *introducing* their essays in ways that invite, intrigue, indicate direction, and guide the reader into the body of the essay;
- for *developing the middle* part of their essays with well-built paragraphs sequenced in a logical way; and

- for *concluding* their essays in a way that summarizes or reflects on what has been written (without repeating it), or perhaps projects onto future considerations without introducing new information, making a call for action supported by reasons already laid out in the body of their essays.

Diagrams, cartoons, and other images can show the structure of an essay and the function of each part. Using them enhances your instruction, making it easier for students to visualize different features of an effective essay. Consider the idea of a train. It is a metaphor to illustrate both purpose and order that makes sense to students living in most geographical settings—city or country, mountain or plains. Show them the engine, the cargo cars, and the caboose. They will get it. (See figure 4.1.)

The engine is the introduction, gets the essay going, and pulls it along; the cargo cars are the body (whatever number needed to carry the information); and the caboose is the conclusion, signaling that the essay has ended. To see a sample of this train metaphor in slides, check out the companion website for this book at http://teachingenglishlanguagearts.com.

READING TO WRITE

Reading maketh a full man, conference a ready man, and writing an exact man.[2]

—Sir Francis Bacon

Looking back at what they have read is a good way to prepare students for what they are going to write. As the Sir Francis Bacon quotation suggests, when students have read, they are full and are ready to conference and talk with others, and eventually prepared to write with the kind of exact—precise and concise—language that leads to compelling, engaging reading for others. Oddly enough, this idea seems particularly true when teaching students have to write persuasive essays—ones that require writers to understand the audience they are intended to influence, or in the English language arts standards, calls for students to take into consideration not just task and purpose but also

Figure 4.1.   Train couplings signify transitions

audience as they select evidence, decide on language and structure in their writing.

It is worth the time spent looking at motivation in literature already studied this school year to help students understand what causes characters to change, and ways they can use what they observe in their reading when they begin writing. Young teens or inexperienced writers may not have the vocabulary yet but will probably notice and mention that change occurs when the character believes refusing to do something may be dangerous, is illegal or immoral, or may betray someone about whom they care deeply. If your students are ready, share with them this language and these explanations. If not, use general terms you know they will understand.

- Beliefs—what the character or audience accepts as fact—"The temperature is below freezing."
- Attitude—what the character or audience believes about forces outside their control that makes the proposed change favorable/unfavorable or positive/negative based on the character's beliefs. "My parents will never get me a . . . ." "They'd ground me if I did that." "That group never respected us anyway."
- Values—the principles upon which character or audience base their lives: moral codes and belief about what is right or wrong. In many cases, these relate to religion and politics. "It is dishonest to steal, even when you're hungry." "Never nark on a relative." "Our family always votes . . .."

Ask students to return to the readings studied so far to seek out passages showing what the author revealed about the beliefs, attitudes, and values of the characters. Then find out who or what in the story convinced the character that making a change in behavior would be a good, safe, or right thing to do. Remember, in many stories, there are at least three attempts to solve the conflict in which the protagonist is embroiled and usually the third, most difficult attempt involves a values decision.

READING CLASSMATES' WRITING INSPIRES BETTER WRITING

Another strategy for compelling better writing is to have students read and respond to the revised but not final drafts of their classmates. Working on their computers, students can just insert comments but not correct the writing of their peers. Correcting, you will have taught them, is the responsibility of the writer. It is the writer's choice to utilize or ignore the commendations and recommendations made on their compositions.

After modeling the process a couple of times, try this. During one fifty-minute class period, students can receive feedback on their drafts from at least three peers. Each reader focuses on one trait of a classmate's draft.

Project a class list on which students find their own names, skip three, and respond to the next three in the list.

Classmate A: CONTENT sufficient to meet requirements of assignment
Classmate B: STRUCTURE of essay, of paragraphs, of sentences
Classmate C: LANGUAGE, QUALITY OF RESOURCES or EVI-
            DENCE, MUGS (Mechanics, Usage, Grammar, Spelling),
            and so forth.

Sometimes, it may be better to use a version of a SIX-TRAITS writing rubric and organize responses for students to respond to.

Classmate A: Traits 1 and 4
Classmate B: Traits 2 and 5
Classmate C: Traits 3 and 6

Middle school teacher Anne Brown's seventh graders found that this process worked well for them. She reported that students were extremely engaged, and the experienced eye-opening because it helped them recognize their own mistakes. One student commented, "I like the way it was broken into three parts. It was easier to write about just one thing. I think I could give better feedback," and another "I like getting more perspectives." Because multiple students expressed frustration at not having time to finish before the timer rang, Ms. Brown recommends allotting enough time for students to read the complete draft rather than rushing the process. The benefits are worth the time given.

José Luis Cano, relatively new at teaching community college students in southern Texas, reflected that he felt good about the conversations he heard as students read their responses after trying this method of structuring feedback. He posted criteria for discussing writing, and vocabulary to describe the writing process and components of the essays. He noted that modeling the process with comments like "I'm having trouble finding your thesis" or "This looks good, but it can be improved by . . .. " was helpful to his new-to-college adult students.

His students responded with helpful feedback after they saw him modeling it and could see the vocabulary they could use when they talked and wrote about their classmates' writing. Mr. Cano acknowledges that with some groups, it was necessary to step in with a more forceful approach rather than guiding their peer responses. You may find that true the first few times you implement this feedback strategy.

Later in the school year, he developed an acronym, ACRSS, to help his students write more useful thesis statements to guide their own writing as they organized their research and to guide their audience who read or listened to their reporting. ACRSS (pronounced "across") stands for "Answer, Claim, Reasons, Specificity, and So what?" He explained that ACRSS functions as a guideline for creating strong thesis statements for the assignment for which he asked students to craft a thesis statement that

- answers the prompt,
- provides an arguable claim,
- presents reasons for the claim,
- meets specificity for the length of the assignment, and
- relates to an important community issue.

Over the course of the year, you may adapt this acronym or design one that works with the students you are teaching. Go ahead and try it.

PRESENTING ARGUMENTS PRECEDES PERSUADING

A writer needs to know something about the readers to choose facts and use reasons that will be convincing. Most students know this but may not realize it. One of the more effective ways to illustrate this is to ask students to draft a letter persuading their parents, guardians, or supervisors to let the writer do something heretofore forbidden.

This is an audience even the youngest middle school students know how to approach; they understand they must come up with both facts and reasons to get permission to do that forbidden thing and they must not finagle with the facts or use faulty reasoning. Once the youngsters have giggled and guffawed about times they have gotten caught doing either of these things, present a lesson on the ethics of argumentation. Keep it light, but keep it real. You may even share a story of your own.

Then, take them back a couple millennia and embellish your mini-lesson with the classical foundation of the art of rhetoric or honesty in arguing, as attributed to Aristotle. You may find cartoons will keep it simple, while telling the story that for eons, an essential part of a classical education has been learning to argue well. Your students will readily accept as true that writers and speakers who can convince the audience to change are the ones who rise to become leaders in the school, community, nation, and even the world.

The effective writer/speaker is one who knows the audience well, who appeals to their feelings, and who explains with reasons that benefit the individuals in that audience. These writers/orators consistently convince others to change their ways. However, those most respected writers and orators usually are trustworthy, acting with integrity, and are those men and women who resist the temptation to twist evidence and use sloppy reasoning.

UNVEILING ARISTOTLE'S ART OF RHETORIC

Go ahead and use the Greek words *ethos, pathos,* and *logos.* These are premium root words for students to know because they make up many words your students encounter in the academic vocabulary now or will in the future. Additionally, students will feel so sophisticated using them to tell family and friends what they learned in their English class. You probably can find PowerPoint slide presentations online that you can adapt for your middle school or students inexperienced with English.

No need to belabor the point or require students to memorize the definitions of each one. The purpose is to show that what they are studying now has been a part of education curricula since the time of . . . ! Use whatever hyperbolic term for a long, long, long time ago will impress your students—the gladiators, time of Christ, ancient Chinese dynasties, or when Abraham, Mohammed, or the Buddha lived.

Just a couple more steps before sending the students off to write compelling persuasive essays on their own. Bring in print, media, and digital ads to show students ways that they—even your most astute ones—are persuaded to buy clothes, food, games, and sugary drinks. As students view commercials that manipulate prospective customers, they develop an understanding about ethos, pathos, and logos more quickly than simply hearing the terms defined. If time permits, you could present a lesson about fallacies that include bandwagoning, hasty generalization, slippery slope, and appeal to authority that even young teens recognize in advertisements they see online, on TV, and in magazines. (See chapter 8 for lessons on reading media.)

SPARRING TO PRACTICE LISTENING
FOR SOUND ARGUMENTS

Practicing aloud arguments and attempts to persuade is an effective way to prepare students for writing strong, convincing essays. Consider conducting SPARs in class. They are SPontaneous ARguments based on everyday topics, such as which is better, more nutritious, more popular, more useful, more economical, more fun than something else. What should be required or banned?

Two pairs of students debate one another for about ten minutes per topic. They must include facts and not just opinions to be convincing. This is an exciting way to teach presenting, listening, and responding to opposing views on topics appropriate for in class discussion. See lessons on the companion website for this book.

- Team A—Speaker 1 draws a topic from a hat or a bowl, announces it to the class, and then has just a couple of minutes to prepare and then present a case for making a change.
- Team B—Speaker 1, the opposing team, must address each argument presented by the first speaker, and within the two or three minutes, counter each argument with her own.
- Team A—Speaker 2 then offers a rebuttal, or response, to those challenges.
- Team B—Speaker 2 sums up the arguments for that side and calls for action.

The audience decides who presents the more convincing case by voting anonymously on a prepared ballot. Then a second set of students comes to the front, draws, and presents arguments for their topic. Usually, three rounds at a time suffice to demonstrate the value of listening and responding with logical reasons. One structure that may help the SPARers stay on task says as follows:

> *Name* it—What's the problem or issue?
> *Explain* it—Show why this is a problem or issue of concern for the audience.
> *Prove* it—Use factual evidence, not just the opinion of speaker.
> *Conclude* it—"Therefore . . .." State a good reason to consider the alternative view or to make a change.

Students are likely to notice how similar this is to the P.I.E. structure described earlier where writers state their position, offer illustrations that show, exemplify the position, and then explain link(s) between the two. Still, it should not be surprising that it takes several attempts at SPARring for students to learn the structure and stay on task without erupting into side arguments. This is hard work that requires attentive listening and disciplined thinking.

The value of SPARring is that students hear how important it is to counter opposing views without insulting the intelligence of the reader/audience. If the writer/speaker does not appear to respect the fact the other side has valid reasons for holding to those beliefs or behaviors, the reader/audience is likely to close down and stop reading or listening. Be prepared. You may have to admonish your students that volume does not convince; practical solutions do.

Compelling Arguments

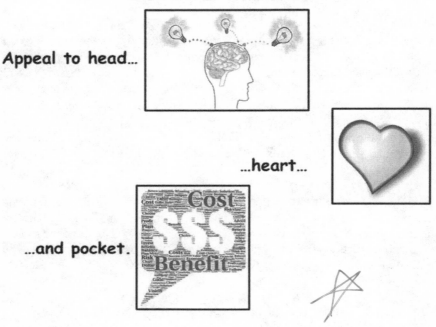

Appeal to head...

...heart...

...and pocket.

WRITING ABOUT ISSUES THAT MATTER

If you would persuade, you must appeal to interest rather than intellect.[3]

—Benjamin Franklin

Students are more enticed to learn when they see an immediate purpose for doing so. It therefore makes sense to assign the persuasive essays in conjunction with current events that take place on your school site, in the community, state, or the world. Culturally sustainable pedagogy encourages teachers to consider culturally relevant topics as often as practical.

A real-world way for students to use their newly crafted skills is to write letters and articles, or create video or podcasts, to persuade someone in authority to change a policy or a law. Students can use the same strategies for writing these letters or articles as they did to write letters to their parents, guardians, or supervisors. Resist the temptation to force the whole class to write about the same topic or on one that is important to you. If they have no passion for the topic, students are likely to resist giving it their all as they plan and create credible essays or performances that answer these kinds of questions:

- What is the problem?
- What does the audience believe or feel about the problem? How do you know?
- What has the audience said or done to show that is what they believe or feel?
- What should be done to solve the problem? How do you know?
- Which arguments will appeal to the head (facts), the heart (emotions), and the pocket (financial cost)?
- Why will a change in belief or action benefit the audience?
- How will life improve once the change is in place?

Now that they have a better understanding of their audience—marshaling their facts, articulating reasons for change, practicing countering arguments—they are ready to write more nuanced essays zoning in on the specific purpose that will compel their readers to take notice, and maybe even, take action.

CONFERENCING TO CLARIFY STUDENT THINKING

No matter how well you have presented lessons, scheduled class time for practice and for review, sometimes only talking to individual students serves to ensure learning. But one-on-one conferencing during the class time is difficult to manage. Planning will help you incorporate this valuable teaching strategy fairly early in the school year. Begin right away modeling ways to respond to writing, then have students work for short periods of time in pairs—reading and responding to drafts; then as small groups in structured read-around-groups; and finally, perhaps by the second quarter, you can begin to integrate in-class conferencing.

When students experience the value of having your unique responses to their writing, they may be patient enough to work independently, reading or writing, while you meet a few students each day in one-on-one conferences. The major reason for holding off scheduling in-class one-on-one conferencing is not due to class management but to have time to build students' confidence in themselves and in one another as reliable readers and peer writing partners. This knowledge prepares them to come to conferences with good questions and open minds. Some teachers require students to confer with three classmates before coming to teacher conference!

In school settings with ready access to technology, either at home or for all students to work on computers simultaneously in class, it is practical to teach students to do online peer responding as you work your way toward one-on-one conferencing. See the earlier description for optional ways to structure such an in-class activity. Until you can manage effective in-class conferencing, consider inviting students who wish to work in this way to meet with you before or after school, or during their study periods. As the word gets around that getting one-on-one feedback from the teacher is helpful, students may be willing to cooperate in class, so they, too, can gain the benefits of this teaching/learning opportunity.

It will take time to teach students how to use class time efficiently, so plan carefully and keep working toward this goal. Commend them when they do well with pairs and small group responding; continue to model and expect their cooperation. Often, they respond just as they should.

Prepping for One-On-One Conferences

How do you prepare students for conferencing so that they will bring some insight to their own reading or writing process and remain open to taking something valuable from the discussion? One strategy is to have students come with specific, written questions based on the assignment guidelines. After they have done in-class prewriting to prime the pumps, have them write first drafts to explore and organize their ideas, using the grading rubric to read and revise. Next, they can participate in some form of peer feedback task and write a second revision. It may then be soon enough to schedule in-class conferences.

If you get involved too soon, students may think all they have to do is follow your advice and earn an A. That erroneous idea seldom is the case when you use the General Grading Guidelines for which an A is awarded for the student's own creative touch. You can teach a B and acknowledge an A. See the General Grading Guideline diagram in chapter 1.

Do you wonder what the rest of the class should be doing while you conduct one-on-one conferences? Depending on the make-up of class and what other assignments students have for the course, students could be doing independent reading, listening to audiobooks, or working on their own drafts or revisions. Early in the term, you may only be able to use a portion of the period for conferences. Once the students become accustomed to them, you may be able to use the majority of the period because students are coming prepared to work and wait. By then, they are less uncomfortable with quiet on their side of the room, and less distracted by the hushed conversation at the teacher's desk.

In your setting, waiting until after students receive their graded paper may be a more propitious time to hold conferences. In this case, students would come to the conference with one section of the paper revised and be prepared to explain how their revision improves their paper. It is not necessary to change the grade on the original essay. Instead, encourage students to use what they learn in the conference when writing the next paper. Writing conferences themselves need not be graded, but simply acknowledged with a check or plus in your grade book. They should serve as a formative assessment, a tool to help you learn more about ways students view their own writing and approach revision.

You soon find keeping some notes about these one-to-one meetings provides good information for parent conferences and questions from administrators, too. Time, patience, modeling, adapting, and adjusting by both the students and the teacher ultimately lead to productive in-class conferencing. Having specific information about each student demonstrates your attention to individuals that all three value: students, parents, and administrators.

TRAINING FOR SUCCESS

The first quarter at most schools is much like spring training for baseball teams. It is not that the athletes do not know the rules or no longer have the physical prowess to play the game; they have not had to utilize that knowledge or those muscles during the off-season. In much the same way, teachers find themselves reviewing and reteaching what they know students have been taught before, not because the students do not know, but because they have not been using what they had learned. You know that for yourself.

When you prepare to teach a lesson, you review details about general topics you have known for years. What's the adage? If they don't use it, they'll lose it. So go ahead and reteach, and then begin to hold the students accountable for using what they are learning again.

ASSESSING WRITING: INFORMALLY OR FORMALLY?

Periodically during the school year teachers are required to assess student learning and submit the results to people outside the classroom. In some schools, this reporting is done totally in-house with only administrators, parents, and students seeing the results. In other school settings, there are state exams, and for many, there are standardized tests that impact the ratings of the school and the evaluation of the teachers. The question arises, "How can teachers prepare and inspire students to write their best in any testing situation?" No easy answer. As often is the case, the kind of preparation depends on the reason for testing.

Students usually write well when they know what is expected. The challenge is to resist making the content so specific that there is little room for creativity. When you have a choice, design formal writing assessments as opportunities for students to shine. No, this does not mean writing easier tests. It means writing tests that measure, in a variety ways, what you have taught and what students are expected to know.

As you teach your students that writing can be a place to explore what they think, they may not be thrown off when they see a question on a test on a topic that is relatively unfamiliar. Continue to remind your students the different purposes for writing and the different ways writing is a process during which they discover what they want to say and then, under teacher guidance, learn how best to say it.

Since you have very definite skills, you are asked to teach and guide students toward learning and showing what they know about good writing; it may be useful to work backward by asking yourself questions similar to those asked when designing long-term writing units and short-term individual lessons.

- What *skills* are you trying to measure in this assessment? Is it how well they understand the texts and topics you've studied together, how well they can show what they know about analyzing a character or a piece of writing, or how well they can write, organize, and develop their response?
- What will you need to *see* in their answers or writing to know their level of understanding or skill? Is it reference to the text? Use of literary language? Organization, development of ideas, and correct use of vocabulary and grammar?

If it is all these, consider some step-by-step test preparation during which students

- review the literary language you've been teaching (direct/indirect characterization, motivation, elements of fiction, text structures, or whatever you have been teaching).
- work together going back to the text to find examples of each of the devices/terms which students save in their notes.
- talk together and share their notes. Those with no notes can work together to create them. It is surprising how much some students recall without having to record what they see and hear. However, none should be allowed to mooch.

As you listen to their talk, you gain insight into what students know or what you may need to help them review.

If you know the formal assessments will require writing single or multiple paragraph responses, let them practice in class, but without pressuring them with grades. The goal is to help them learn to use time wisely. Remember the story that began this chapter?

As you teach them how to begin responding to essay questions, invite them to write a statement of opinion about the topic you assign in which they

- use some kind of modifier to indicate how well or poorly they think the author has developed the characters,
- explain how much the student can identify with the characters, and
- show how they see connections to everyday incidents in the way one or more characters act or react in the book.

Their essay will then be an attempt to show why that modifier is true/valid.

Then begin writing P.I.E. paragraphs in which they state their position or opinion, illustrate with examples from the beginning, middle, and end of the book, and explain ways those illustrations support their position/opinion. This explanation is the most important element because it shows their level of understanding.

The students should be ready to write an introduction leading into their body paragraph(s) and a conclusion paragraph to reflect or summarize what they've written.

Occasionally, practice within the same time constraints under which the students will be tested. Ask them to write a reflection on how they used the time. Did they finish? Are they satisfied with the results? What can they do differently to use the time more efficiently?

Rather than show them a fully polished sample essay, plan to write along with them, and then show how you build your essay. Ultimately, students come to understand how to organize and develop a basic essay within a pre-scribed time period. Knowing this is a different kind of writing for a different purpose should reduce their anxiety about having no time for multiple revisions and deep editing. Some students are relieved to know they can write the introduction last! It is not when the introduction is written, but when the reader reads it. Just save space on the top of their paper to come back and write that inviting opening passage.

Keep it light. The purpose is for them to understand how to pace themselves, so they can complete the tasks to the best of their ability. Resist the temptation to burden them—or you—with the impact of test results. Encourage them to do their best.

WEIGHTING AND GRADING WRITING

Unfortunately, middle school students, like their counterparts in high school and college, often are more concerned about the grades they are earning than

The school year journey has ups and downs

what they are learning. To reduce attention paid to grades, consider giving low weight to grades in the first quarter, and during the school year incrementally increase the impact on reported grades. This does not mean lowering the demands on the assignments. Instead, for example, assign just 30 points for final drafts during the first quarter; 50 during the second quarter; 75 during the third quarter; and then 100 points during the fourth quarter. As the semester progresses, students still are being held accountable for writing well, but are not penalized as they learn.

Include in each assignment a rubric that includes the minimum that is expected in terms of content, organization, and correctness for each grade or point level. The students will see what is required, will ask questions when they do not understand, and usually will be less disappointed with their grades when they do not earn the highest ones. This done? Move on. Good teaching inspires pride in performance. Trust yourself and your students to delight in doing well.

CONCLUSION

It may take several weeks to make the trip from reviewing informative writing to teaching persuasive writing. For some teachers, it takes the three quarters of the school year. However, if you know where you are heading, the expedition does not seem interminable, if you are confident that you have not gotten lost.

Stop occasionally to rest and enjoy the side trips that confirm the value of teaching different modes of writing. Look at ways published writers and speakers use the skills you are teaching. Invite students to bring in examples they see in other classes, in their own independent reading, or even to point them out in the fiction and nonfiction you study together. Craft lessons for students to model what they read and view.

This does not mean, however, that you will never have to review or remind students of what they know. What they remember, students are likely to implement when they write themselves. What they are trying themselves, they are likely to notice and point out during peer-editing sessions. So, what they discover with your guidance is more lasting and useful than what they are simply shown or told.

By the final quarter of the school year, on the last few miles of the journey, the students become more confident and competent persuasive writers and speakers because they understand the purpose of different kinds of writing and speaking. They appreciate the ethics of argumentation, the value of organization, and the importance of respecting their reader/audience to become effective communicators. Equally important, your maturing writers will have become more critical readers and listeners, more aware of ways that others may use these skills to convince their readers/listeners/viewers to change their beliefs and behavior.

Finally, by including this range of lessons and varied assessments, you will have reached your destination, meeting many of the standards for English language arts for your assigned curriculum. And as a bonus, if you include publishing work, collecting photographs, and creating videos, you all will have souvenirs to share from this successful and rewarding journey of teaching and learning together.

NOTES

1. Blaise Pascal, Brainy Quote, 2009. https://www.brainyquote.com/quotes/blaise_pascal_133403 (accessed January 2, 2018).
2. Francis Bacon, "Essays of Francis Bacon—Of Studies," Authorama Public Domain Books, n.d. http://www.authorama.com/essays-of-francis-bacon-50.html (accessed January 2, 2018).
3. Benjamin Franklin, Finest Quotes, n.d. http://izquotes.com/quote/283028 (accessed January 2, 2018).

Chapter 5

Taking T.I.M.E. to Teach Poetry

Words, Words, Words
Words stir me
When I hear them,
When I read them,
When I write them,
When I speak them.

Words urge me
To keep listening
To keep reading
To keep writing
To keep speaking.

Let me hear you,
so I can know you.
Let me speak,
so you can know me.

Prodigiously stirring words
help me know you.
And viscerally urging words
help me know me.

—Anna Roseboro "Words, Words, Words"

For some reason, young teens are apprehensive about studying poetry. They believe there is a key or secret code to understanding this genre of literature and only teachers have the key to decipher that code. Experienced readers know that is not the case; it is a matter of understanding the genre and

Teaching poetry can be challenging

approaching poetry in a different way—paying special attention to poets' careful selection and arrangement of words. The lessons in this chapter are designed to provide you and your students with a set of strategies that can help them approach, read, understand, analyze, write in the style of, and write about classical, contemporary, structured, and free-verse poetry. Students will be reading closely and developing those standards for English language arts anchor skills relating to reading, writing, speaking, listening, and viewing, while using technology for learning, publishing, and showing what they know.

PREPARING TO TEACH POETRY

Scrounge as many books of poetry as you can. Look for them at the school or neighborhood library, your department library, and borrow from your colleagues. If several of you are teaching poetry at the same time, you may wish to borrow a library cart so you can merge your poetry collections and move the cart easily among your rooms. To make this a really rich experience for your students, have a ready trove of poems for students to mine during this course of study. If your students have access to technology at home or at school, assemble a list of age-appropriate websites to post in a hyperlinked list on your web page so students can access them quickly. Even if you are in a high-tech setting, lots of print books should still be available in your classroom. There's just something visceral about holding and reading a book in print.

Finding a Poem to Introduce the Genre of Poetry

This first day is a good time to talk about the value of multiple readings and why it often is necessary for this condensed form of literature. The "Unfolding Bud" by Naoshi Koriyama is a great conversation starter. In this poem, Koriyama compares reading a poem to watching a water lily bud unfold—it takes time, but the wait is worth it.

You may project the poem or hand out copies, but at first, do not read the poem aloud. Instead, without saying anything more, let the students look at it for a couple of minutes. Sometimes silence gives space for student learning.

Then, use a multiple readings format. Here is how it works. Ask the students to read the poem silently, paying attention to the punctuation and marking words or phrases that catch their attention. Next, read the poem aloud yourself. Then, ask them to do a "jump-in" oral reading. One student begins reading and stops at the first mark of punctuation (comma, semicolon, period, question mark, etc.). Another student, without raising his or her hand, continues reading until the next punctuation mark.

Students are likely to giggle when more than one student begins reading aloud at the same time. Just start over and encourage students who jump in at the same time to listen to each other and read together as one voice. It usually takes three or four false starts before the students get the idea and are comfortable reading aloud this way.

Other students can continue jumping in to read until the end of the poem. Relax and allow the pauses between readers to be moments of resonation and reflection. False starts encourage students to pay attention to the words, lines, and punctuation, and thus expand their understanding of the poem. One more jump reading, this time stopping at the end of each line usually will suffice to make the point. Multiple readings expand and deepen understanding.

When teaching poetry, resist the temptation to ask students what the poem "means." This phrase erroneously suggests there is only one meaning for a poem. The phrase "what it says" encourages the students to look at the individual words and respond with a literal meaning, which can be the first step to analyzing poetry. The subsequent steps include determining whether the poem is saying something about a bigger issue or idea and whether the poem is speaking metaphorically.

A poem may have been written simply to recreate a very personal incident, observation, or experience. Yet, when read by others, the poem speaks to the readers about issues quite different from the literal ideas originally intended. Often these bigger, universal ideas do not emerge or manifest themselves on the first or second readings. "Unfolding Bud" closes with the lines "over and over again," which suggests that this genre is somewhat different from some prose and drama in that, often, multiple readings are required to understand poetry.

Some poets, like Quincy Troupe, are very aware that poems can be seen to mean lots more than the words on the page. Share with your students these excerpted stanzas from, "My Poems Have Holes Sewn into Them" Have fun with the unusual way the words seem to be organized. Note particularly the last words in each line, the punning, and the use of the ampersand sign instead of the word, "and." How do these visual choices impact the reading? (Won't "ampersand" be fun to teach your middle school students?)

> my poems have holes sewn into them
> & they run, searching for light
> at the end of tunnels, they become trains
> or at the bottom of pits, they become blackness
> or in the broad, winging daylight
> they are words that fly
> . . .
>
> my poems have holes sewn into them
> & their voices are like different keyholes
> through which dumb men search for speech, blind
> men search for sight
> words, like drills, penetrating sleep
> keys unlocking keyholes of language
> words giving sight to blind peoples eyes
> . . .
>
> my poems have holes sewn into them
> & they are spaces between worlds
> are worlds themselves
> words falling off into one another
> colliding, like people gone mad, they space out
> fall, into bottomless pits, which are black
> holes of letters that become words
> & worlds, like silent space
> between chords of a piano

—Quincy Troupe, "My Poems Have Holes Sewn into Them"[1]

Reading Poems in Different Ways

If you would rather not use "jump-in" reading to introduce the unit, slowly read the poem aloud yourself, allowing time for the words to make their impact. Then ask a student to read the poem according to the punctuation, rather than just stopping at the end of each line. This second reading helps the students focus on the fact that poems sometimes include punctuation that serves the same functions as that used in prose. Punctuation clarifies the meaning of words organized in a chosen order. It still is beneficial to have a third reading of the poem by another student who, by this time, may have an idea of what the poet may be trying to express. This student may choose to emphasize different words or reads at a different pace and thus offers a third level of understanding. Either approach—jump-in reading or multiple readings—demonstrates the value of repetition to allow a poem to reveal itself to the readers and listeners.

DEFINING POETRY: A FOUNDATION FOR DISCUSSION

Now, on the first day of the unit, is a prime time to provide students with a definition of poetry, a distinctive genre of literature that sometimes baffles new readers and at other times thrills them with its versatility. Use the definition in your anthology or the one that follows; dictate the definition, and then have the students write the definition in the poetry section they have set up in their paper or electronic journals.

Definition: "Poetry is literature designed to *convey* a vivid and imaginative sense of experience, especially by the use of *condensed* language *chosen* for its sound and *suggestive* power as well as for its meaning and by the use of such literary devices as *structured* meter, *natural cadences*, rhyme, and metaphor."[2]

You may want to read the definition a couple of times, letting your voice emphasize the italicized words. Then, dictate it slowly so students can write the definition in their journals. Afterward, project the definition so students can verify their writing. Why this laborious start? Hearing, listening, writing, and viewing are ways to reinforce the concept. This definition will form the basis of subsequent reflections on the form and function of poetry studied throughout the unit. Having a definition aids close reading and deeper understanding of the genre, as well as how to make sense of it when students begin to experiment with writing it.

Take a few moments more and ask students what they think the italicized words mean in the context of poetry. If no one offers definitions, direct the students to look up the words and to share appropriate definitions with the class.

Now return to the poem "Unfolding Bud" or "My Poems Have Holes Sewn into Them" and ask the students what they imagine either poem is saying to them about reading poetry. What elements of the definition have Koriyama and Troupe used in their poems?

To solidify student understanding, end the lesson by having the students read aloud in unison the definition of poetry they have written in their notebooks, and then, like a Greek chorus, read one of the opening poems. The left side of the class can read stanza one; the right side, stanza two, and in unison, the whole class can read stanza three. What power!

SWIMMING AROUND IN POEMS

For homework, you can assign the students to peruse their literature anthology or other poetry collections they have, can borrow, and find in the library or online. Ask them to read four or five poems, list the titles and authors of those poems they like, and then handwrite into their notebook at least one poem they particularly like.

If such an assignment is not a realistic expectation for your students, allot in-class time for them to look through their anthology or the poetry books you have collected for their use in the classroom. Just ask each student to select and copy into his or her own notebook one or two poems that attract their attention. Handwriting is heuristic, so insist, but don't badger.

For those reading online, encourage them to key in the poem rather than simply copying and pasting. The physical act of handwriting or keying in the poem slows students down a bit so they can pay attention to individual words, line structure, and the pattern in the poem, three of the distinguishing features of this genre of literature.

Your students then have self-selected poem(s) to refer to and share with the class later during the unit. The value is that students are reading a variety of poems for which they are required to do nothing more than choose one they like. And the bonus? They are likely to read twice as many poems than if you were to assign a specific one to read for class. The goal here is to get them reading poetry and to become more at ease with this literary form. The next class meeting, simply record in the grade book whether each student has poem(s).

 ## USING POPULAR SONG LYRICS TO EXPLORE POETRY

Encourage students to bring in song lyrics that are appropriate for sharing in class. Until you point it out, probably few young adolescents recognize that song lyrics often are poems. Having your students bring in song lyrics and poems of their choice also is a way for you to become more familiar with what they listen to and find interesting. Students also feel they are a part of the learning process because their choices help to shape the lessons. Depending on your students, you may wish to collect and read the lyrics first, then use them for a lesson later in the unit. Remember to incorporate as many of theirs as you can. Some students may want to bring in ten-to-fifteen-second musical samples of the choruses for their selected song lyrics. Play a few of these as examples of poetic repetition.

SHARING POETRY T.I.M.E.:
A STRATEGY FOR POETRY ANALYSIS

Poetry T.I.M.E. is an idea for poetry analysis passed along from teacher to teacher across the nation for decades. You may have been taught a similar way and find this clever acronym just what you need to organize your instruction and enhance student learning. You may even have former students return to express their appreciation for having a mnemonic that serves them well on standardized and placement tests, as well as on final exams in other courses. In relation to poetry, T.I.M.E. stands for title, thoughts, and theme; imagery; music; and emotion.

UNDERSTANDING POETRY

TAKES T.I.M.E.

T = the POET'S TITLE
       THOUGHT(S) / THEME(S)
I = IMAGERY
M = MUSIC
E = EMOTION PERIOD

(Illustration by Nabeel Usmani)

Knowing this acronym can help students unlock meaning in poetry. As your students have learned in their readings of the Koriyama and Troupe selections, poems are written in condensed language and often require multiple readings. The T.I.M.E. really is a pun and refers not only to the fact that it often takes more time to read and write poetry but also to elements of a poem that, when considered independently, can lead to a deeper understanding of the poem in its entirety. Taking T.I.M.E. for poetry will help them recognize the holes poets like Quincy Troupe may have conscientiously or unconsciously sewn into their poems.

The Letter "T"

Begin with T, for the title of a poem. If a poet has chosen a title, it often hints to what the poem is about and may indicate the emotion or opinion the poet has about the experience related in the poem. The title may be a peephole into the interior the reader will explore once inside the poem. The T also could stand for

T

TITLE

THOUGHT(S)

THEME(S)

"T" of T.I.M.E.

(Illustration by Nabeel Usmani)

the thoughts or theme of the poem. T.I.M.E. is a flexible acronym, and you can decide the best word(s) to use with the students you have. You may use one, two, or three of these T words. All are related to the study of poetry.

Just for fun, project a copy of this poem "Finalists" by Nancy Genevieve. Do not show the students the title when you ask them what the poem is about. Then, show them the title and ask how their understanding of the poem changes.

"Finalists"

Seven turkey vultures
   on the uppermost gable
   of the cow barn

preening.[3]

Ask students to look at the poem they have written in their journals. How might meaning be changed if there was no title?

Next, draw the students' attention to concepts about the speaker and audience. Published poetry is meant to be understood. You may choose to clarify this idea and specify "published poetry" because many people write poetry just for themselves and may not care whether anyone else even reads it, let alone understands it. Generally, though, a poet is someone saying something to someone.

That first someone is "the speaker" who may or may not be the poet. For example, you may have an elderly woman who writes a poem in the persona of an adolescent boy. Though the poet is a woman, the speaker in the poem is a boy. Looking at the kind of pronouns used, the vocabulary and images help readers imagine the audience. One visual way to help students think of poetry as a piece of writing with a message is to use a graphic design with three spaces—one large rectangle in the middle of the page and small circle on the left and a larger one on right of the large rectangle.

After they make this full-page chart in the poetry section of their journals, ask students to draw a picture of a possible speaker in the small circle on the left and in the larger circle on the right, a possible audience: one person, a special person, or a group of people. Then, in the rectangle in the center, they could write a summary of what the poem could be saying and quote a couple of lines from the poem to support their opinion.

Demonstrate how this could work by referring first to "My Poems Have Holes Sewn into Them" by Quincy Troupe and then to "Unfolding Bud" by Naoshi Koriyama. Draw the graphic organizer on the board and then ask students, "Who could be the speaker?" "Who could be the audience?" For the Koriyama poem, typical answers include a parent talking to a frustrated student, persuading the young person to hang in and not give up just because the poem is difficult to understand after one or two readings. Some students may say it is a teacher speaking to an individual student or to the whole class.

POETRY IS

SOMEONE saying SOMETHING to *SOMEONE(s)

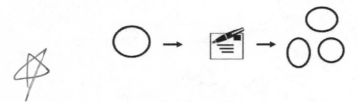

*a specific individual, kind of person, group of people

Poetry is meant to be understood

To reinforce the ideas of speaker and audience, distribute a copy of Emily Dickinson's poem, "I'm Nobody." You could ask students to imagine this is to be spoken by a character in a play or in a movie and to think of as many different speaker and audience sets as they can. What could be the setting? Who could be the speaker? Who is the audience? The only limitation is that the sets must be supported by the words of the poem. Your students may come up with combinations or settings such as listed here:

- A student new to the school talking to another student at lunch time
- A new player on an athletic team to another player
- A prisoner talking to another prisoner
- A new teacher at the first department meeting
- A boy at the playground during a pick-up ball game
- A rapper waiting to perform on a TV program
- A girl at a skateboarding competition
- An actress to another actress trying out for a part in a play
- A parent talking to another parent during the school open house
- A woman attending a neighborhood luncheon for the first time

If you are in the mood, act a little silly, ham it up, and reread the poem in the voices and persona of the pairs the students suggest. Great fun! Makes the point, too, of multiple possibilities but common meanings.

The Letter "I"

"I" stands for the imagery of poetry. Poets use words to create pictures, and evoke emotions or memories of incidents, in the minds of readers and

IMAGERY
FIGURATIVE
SENSORY

"I" of T.I.M.E.

(Illustration by Nabeel Usmani)

listeners. Poets may use sensory or figurative imagery or a combination of the two.

Rather than presenting this portion of the lesson as lecture, simply draw or project an eye, an ear, a mouth, a hand, and a nose on the board. Then ask the students to label the drawings and give examples of words or phrases that appeal to the senses. Prepare for the lesson by looking at a variety of poems, compiling sample lines from poems that illustrate appeals to the various senses. Better yet, invite students to offer lines they recall from lyrics of songs familiar to them—but be prepared with your examples just to prime the pump to get them thinking as you remind them that sensory imagery appeals to one or more of the five senses: sight, hearing, taste, touch, and smell. It is through our senses that we experience the world, and many poets appeal to these senses as they recreate their own experiences in poetic form.

This would be a good time to ask students to look back at the poems they selected and copied into their journals at the beginning of the unit. Set your timer for five minutes for students to look at their poem and mark images. Then reset for ten minutes, have students pull their desks together, or turn to a table partner and share these poems, pointing out examples of sensory images from their chosen verses. Working with poems they have chosen validates the assignment to choose and copy them into their notebooks. Invite volunteers to read to the class lines that illustrate the sensory images they find. Variety spices the lessons and increases interest.

Next, direct their attention to figurative imagery. Many middle school students have learned about *similes* and *metaphors* in earlier grades and are able to define them for the class. Some know *personification*; fewer students recall or were taught *hyperbole*, *symbol*, and *allusion*. Be prepared to introduce or review these devices and give students definitions and examples. Here are some simple ones of these types of figurative imagery:

- *Simile*: a comparison between two things using "like" or "as." Example: The thunder roared like a bear.
- *Metaphor*: an implied comparison between two things without using the words "like" or "as." Example: Dime-sized raindrops pelted me in the face.
- *Hyperbole*: exaggeration to create an effect. Example: That goldfish is as big as my leg!
- *Personification*: giving a non-human thing the characteristics of a person. Example: The dog smirked and snatched up my sandwich.

Occasionally a poet uses a *symbol*—something concrete that stands for something else: an abstract concept, another thing, idea, or event. For example, a "flag" is a cloth on a stick. But a certain configuration of colors and shapes such as stars on a blue rectangular field in the upper left corner of a red and white striped cloth suggests the American flag, which stands for the nation, for freedom, and for patriotism.

Symbols can be a great opening to talk about cultural contexts, too. For example, a snake or serpent symbolizes different ideas depending on the culture, the religion, or the nation. Red in some cultures is a sad color representing blood or anger; in other cultures, it is a happy color representing marriage or royalty.

An *allusion* is the reference to another body of literature, a movie, or an incident the writer believes the readers know. Allusions can help writers create an image with just a few words because the writers trust the allusion to trigger memories, ideas, or emotions from its reference in the poem. Your students may enjoy playing with this poetic device in much the same way Nancy Genevieve has in these few lines from her poem "A Kiss."

> Enchanted innocent kissed the frog
> and heard only a croak in reply.
>
> Will you, child, kiss it again
> and give him another try?

Or will you release him
        and then begin to cry?
Or worse,

        will you never ever
        give another frog a chance?[4]

In Western literature, frequently allusions are made to the Bible with its Hebrew and Christian Scriptures; Roman and Greek mythology; Shakespeare's writings; and fairy tales. Sometimes a reference may be made to a familiar movie or a historical incident like *Star Wars*, the Civil War or the Gold Rush. If your students represent a range of cultures and national origins, select samples from the literature and historical events that are more familiar to them. Consider stories, myths, and sacred texts your students may know from literature and life in Central and South America, Asia, India, Africa, and Australia. Better yet, invite them to bring in examples.

You could spend the remainder of the period looking at examples of poems that have strong imagery. Project poems already discussed in class. Ask students to find examples of the kinds of images to share and compare with a partner, and encourage them to copy favorite lines into their journals. Remember, to find their own examples, the students read much more poetry than if you provide all the examples. Equally important is the fact that each year you teach the unit you should be learning, looking forward to discovering poems that interest students in each different class.

Students might enjoy pointing out the figurative language in the poems that follow. Notice the ways that Nancy Genevieve uses metaphors and personification in her poems, "Evening Cicadas" and "The Pond."[5]

        Evening cicadas
            tune up for night
            practicing their lull-a-bye
            for summer.

This short poem illustrates so well the personification that can bring such a personal appeal to a poem. What images do your students notice in this next one?

        Bubbles frozen in ice
            pearls of silence,
            waiting for spring.

        Crystals etched in glaze
            petals of illusion,
            blooming by night.

          Twilight bathed in mist
             flames of fading,
          seeping into no more.

PATTERNING POETRY:
TEACHER AND STUDENT RESPONSES

An assignment that always evokes positive responses and pretty good poetry is one on patterning poems. Ask the students to select one or two of the poems that they particularly like either from their anthology or from one of the books in your room. Next, ask them to visualize a memorable experience of their own. Finally, invite them to pattern the structure and imagery of one of their chosen poems to recreate the experience of that incident. Of course, if you are writing poems along with them (and you should), you experience what it feels like to write on demand as you are asking them to do. Then you, too, have something newly written to read during sharing time.

The Letter "M"

"M" stands for music or the sounds in poetry. According to the definition used earlier, poets chose words "for their sound and suggestive power." Look at three aspects of music and poetry: rhythm, rhyme, and the sound of words. Some poets arrange their words to create a pattern of beats or *rhythm*. If your students are ready, teach the ITADS, an acronym for five common poetic rhythm patterns—iambic, trochaic, anapestic, dactylic, and spondee. These words identify the patterns of stressed and unstressed syllables, information students surely are expected to know and use in high school.

During this lesson on music, mention to the students that ITADS patterns are called the "feet" of poetry. There is only one stressed syllable in each foot. Explain that a poem's rhythm or the "meter" is named for the number of feet or beats per line and the kind of foot that is in each line. For example, a line of poetry with four feet or four beats is tetrameter (*tetra* Greek for four). If the feet are iambic—one unstressed syllable followed by a stressed one—the line is identified as iambic tetrameter. Have fun by asking students to identify the rhythm patterns of their own names. Anna is trochaic. Jamar is iambic. Small is spondee. Roseboro is dactylic. What are the patterns of your name?

Moving to the Music of Poetry

Because many students are kinesthetic learners and can remember what they feel physically, you should demonstrate the rhythms of poetry that way, too.

How about inviting students to clap their hands, tap one foot, or snap their fingers to the beat? Read a poem with a strong beat while the students are standing up and marching in place.

To use that abundance of adolescent energy, have the students march around the room when you read William Wordsworth's "Daffodils": "I wander'd lonely as a cloud." Rather than wandering quietly, stomp loudly. Or, use your arms to sway broadly from side to side to show the rhythm of the waves in John Masefield's "Sea Fever": "I *must* go down to the seas again, to the *lonely* sea and the sky." Of course, the students see right away the rhythm of song lyrics, but you could save this until later. For now, acknowledge that "Just as some poetry has a specific rhythm pattern, so do the lyrics or words of some songs you know."

A second way to look at the music of poetry is to consider the *rhyme*, which occurs when words with similar sounds are used in an observable pattern. The rhyme may occur at the end of a line or within it. Students can discover the pattern of rhyme by using letters of the alphabet to indicate repeated sounds. For example, begin writing the letter "a" at the end of the first line of poetry. If the second line ends with the same sound, write "a" again. If it ends with

(Illustration by Nabeel Usmani)

a different sound, change to "b." Continue throughout the poem to determine if there is a pattern and what the pattern is.

The narrative poem "The Cremation of Sam McGee" by Robert W. Service makes particularly interesting reading when you are teaching internal and end rhyme. The macabre story is intriguing, too. Check out the online versions by Robert Service and Johnny Cash who have recorded renditions of this narrative poem. Your students may enjoy the photos, too.

Point out that free and blank verse poetry have no systematic rhyme pattern. You probably plan to discuss this kind of poetry later in your unit, but should mention it out now, particularly if students bring in examples of free verse poetry or notice it in their class anthology. This is why it is good to begin the unit with the definition of poetry that mentions structured meter or natural cadences. Your discussion of the music of poetry gives space to talk about blank and free verse without having to provide another definition or having to back pedal when students point out that some poetry is unstructured in terms of rhythm and rhyme.

Seeing Song Lyrics as Poetry

Now is an optimal time to ask selected students to read aloud the lyrics of their favorite songs. Most of them have a steady beat and many of them rhyme, making more concrete the connection between poetry of music and poetry in books. Be prepared for students to show more interest in what they bring to class. Show your enthusiasm as you look at and listen to what they bring. They are providing you a window into their worlds; what you learn reveals what they know, and what you may need to teach or reteach as you continue planning learning experiences for your poetry unit. Combine the familiar with the new by encouraging your students to use the vocabulary of poetry as they talk about poems they choose themselves.

If you have the nerve of most middle school teachers, you can "prove" the link between poetry and music by singing the "I'm Nobody" poem to either "Yellow Rose of Texas" or "America, the Beautiful"! Even if you are a very good singer, the students probably are going to laugh at you, but they also remember the lesson. Is that not the goal of teaching?

A third way to talk about the music or sound of poetry is to point out *onomatopoeia*, words that are spelled to imitate the sound they describe.

Middle school students love making peculiar, sometimes shocking and vulgar, noises. One way to exploit that particular pleasure is to have students write poems that capture the sounds of everyday experiences. Warren, a seventh grader, wrote "The Kitchen" about the sounds at home. Like Shakespeare, Warren enjoys making up words, too.

With a cling clang
Not a bang or dang
a swish and a wish
all the dishes are in the sink
screech creach
open
close
scuffles ruffles
a sea of bubbles and water
a crounging rounging
with a turn of the knob
all the dishes are clean
then click click click
whoosh.
Are you hungry for lunch yet?

Another way to address sound as you discuss the music of poetry is to consider repetition of vowels (*assonance*) or consonants (*consonance* or *alliteration*). Most students recognize tongue twisters as examples of alliteration.

Students are intrigued to learn that the sound of words suggests certain emotions, too. For example, a poet who wishes to convey the emotion or sense of experience in a calm, peaceful way is likely to select words with soft-sounding consonants like l, m, n, and the sibilant s. If the memory is unpleasant or bitter, the poet is likely to pick words with hard consonants that must be forced through the lips and teeth to be formed, like p, t, f, or guttural sounds like k, g, j, and the z sounding s.

A graphic way to illustrate this can be pointing out that most obscene words in English have harsh, guttural, and dental sounds. Of course, you need not say them aloud or write them down. Students know the words if you refer to the "F" word or the "S" word. Students smile and smirk, and your point is made. If many of your students speak other languages, and if you can maintain control of the class, you may ask these students if profane words in their language follow this pattern of harsh sounds. Again, let them think, but not speak the words. The point is made.

The Letter "E"

The "E" stands for the emotion of the poem—the emotion expressed by the poet and the emotion experienced by the reader. How do students discover these emotions? By paying attention to the kinds of images (comparisons to positive or negative things), and the music, rhyme, rhythm, and sounds of the words the poet chooses to use to convey the experience of the poem. Sometimes a poet's message is revealed in the layout of the words on the page.

The students may find examples of emotions expressed such as pride, love, grief/distress, fear, joy, jealousy, or shame/embarrassment. They may experience similar feelings as they read or hear the poems, but the emotion expressed and experienced often is not the same! Have them try their new analyzing skills reading and talking about "The Boy in the Window" by Richard Wilbur.

If the students are ready, teach them that the "tone" of a poem refers to the author's attitude or feeling about the topic or experience related in the poem. On the other hand, "mood" refers to the way the poem makes the reader feel when he or she reads or hears a poem. To help make the link more personal, you can draw their attention to the M in mood and say, "Mood means the way

EMOTION

TONE

EXPRESSED BY THE POET

EXPRESSED by POET
EXPERIENCED by READER / LISTENER

MOOD

EXPERIENCED by READER / LISTENER

"E" of T.I.M.E.

(Illustration by Nabeel Usmani)

the poem makes ME, the reader, feel." That usually is sufficient instruction at this time. As you teach these poetry terms, continue to encourage students to use them regularly when talking and writing about poetry. Such use raises the level of their conversation and expands their working vocabulary. Makes them feel oh so sophisticated!

WRITING ABOUT POETRY, TELLING THE T.I.M.E.

Consider creating a handout or set of slides to guide students to tell the T.I.M.E. about poetry as they discuss it with classmates and before they begin writing about what they understand about poems you assign for analysis. Include such prompts as follows:

- T = Title, Thought, and Theme

What does the title suggest? Who could be the speaker? Who could be the audience? In your opinion, what is a message?

- I = Imagery and Figurative Language

What *kind(s)* of imagery are used? What words or lines support your answer?

- M = Music and Sound

   If there is a rhythm pattern, mark the poem: use stressed "/" and unstressed "u" marks to show rhythm pattern. What kind of rhythm pattern is in this poem? On the poem, use "abc's" to show rhyme scheme. What special kinds of words or techniques does the author use to create sound for effect in this poem? What words prove your answer?

- E = Emotion (expressed/experienced)

   What emotion is expressed by the poet in this poem? What words or lines support your answer? What emotion do you experience as the reader of this poem? What words, phrases, or lines evoke this emotional response? How well does this poem reflect our definition of poetry? (See journal for exact wording).

T.I.M.E. MNEMONIC

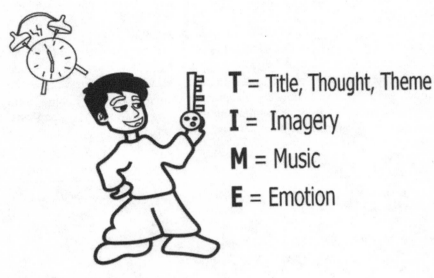

T = Title, Thought, Theme

I = Imagery

M = Music

E = Emotion

(Illustration by Nabeel Usmani)

SPENDING T.I.M.E. READING POEMS INDEPENDENTLY

One way for students to practice reading on their own without feeling undue pressure is to ask them to continue bringing in poems and to point out the ways their self-selected poems reflect the various elements already studied. This subtly entices them to read more widely. They are likely to return to the books skimmed before and come across poems that speak to them differently this time.

Giving this assignment again also reveals to you how students' choice of poetry is being modified by the series of lessons you are teaching. Invite them to post their choices in your class online folder, remembering to include the title, author, and source. Or they can print out copies and staple those on a bulletin board set aside for this purpose in your classroom, labeled "Poems We Like."

As they seek out poems, encourage your students to interview their family members to learn about their favorites. It's surprising how amazed middle school students are to learn that their moms, dads, aunts, uncles, and even grandparents had to memorize and recite poetry as a regular part of their literature coursework! If your students speak languages other than English at home, invite them to bring in poems by favorite poets in those languages and read them aloud to the class. This affirms their heritage and expands the cultural experience for you and their classmates as well.

Allow plenty of class time for students to immerse themselves in the poetry you assemble in the classroom, in their anthology, and on the websites. Those students who have not done so before may now choose to bring in lyrics from their favorite songs—appropriate ones, of course! Consider including an assignment for students to recite a suitable poem of their choice.

Alert your students to the fact that the poems address an array of topics in a variety of ways. Remind your eager learners to use their judgment on which poems would be appropriate to share in class. Thankfully, by this time in the school year, you have established a classroom milieu for sensitive reading and sensible selections. However, reminding them at this time is still a good idea.

Notice in textbox 5.1, the use of "a message or theme" is to keep the poem open for the students to draw from it what the poem says to them. As soon

---

TEXTBOX 5.1:   WRITING ABOUT POETRY
Complete the Analysis by
Telling the T.I.M.E. of the Poem

Introduction

A. What is most memorable idea, image, or literary device you recall about the poem? What direct quotation from the poem would be an effective attention getter?
B. State the title and author of the poem.
C. State your thesis—what ideas will you have in each paragraph?

Body

A. What is the poem about? Consider **T.** information.
B. What is the structure of the poem? Consider **I.** and **M.** information.
C. Use the literary terms to discuss your response.
D. What is the author's attitude? Your response? Consider **E.** information.

Conclusion

A. Summarize ideas discussed by connecting the structure to the message or your response to the poem.
B. How did the author's use of images and music convey the message and influence your response?

as you suggest the "meaning," your students begin guessing and hoping they come up with the "right" answer. With self-control, you can let the poems speak for themselves.

As you plan to teach poetry in a more formal way, schedule time to assign an extensive poetry project for which students collect and share poems they find and ones they write to practice the various poetic devices you study. See chapter 6 for ideas to adapt or adopt.

CONCLUSION

Few readers deny either that poets tend to write cryptically or that it takes more effort to discover what poets have to say to their listeners and readers. When you teach your students to tell the T.I.M.E. of a poem, you give them a golden key they can use for life. Using this key, they know to look systematically for different aspects of the poem on each reread. They experience delight of discovery and enthusiasm of empowerment when you give them T.I.M.E. to study this genre of literature.

As when traveling in a new country, sampling new and different foods, the students may even develop gustatory joy from sampling this form of literary expression. Through the guided practice you offer, your squirmy, restless students slow down and pay attention to the words, the form, the sounds, and eventually to messages in poetry. They may even astonish you when their careful reading leads to interpretations similar to those that published critics write about the poems!

Your traveling companions are ready to demonstrate how close they are coming to the English language arts anchor standards for reading that recommend students know how to interpret this genre of literature based on the technical traits, figurative meaning, and impact of word choice.[6]

By the end of your formal instruction along this school year journey, your students feel far more confident about studying this challenging literary genre. They may not have the ease of Huck Finn's friend Emmeline Grangerford and be able to "slap down a line . . . just scratch it out and slap down another one,"[7] but they now are able to read, write, and talk more confidently about poetry in their own way. Your students can respond to those "prodigiously stirring words" and feel comfortable putting pen to paper to capture the "viscerally urging words" that become poems of their own.

(Illustration by Nabeel Usmani)

NOTES

1. Quincy Troupe, "My Poems Have Holes Sewn into Them." In *Transcircularities: New and Selected Poems*, 1st ed., edited by Quincy Troupe. (Minneapolis: Coffee House Press, 2002), 98–99.
2. Houghton Mifflin, *Houghton Mifflin College Dictionary*. (Boston: Houghton Mifflin, 1986).
3. Nancy Genevieve, "Finalists." In *American Religion and Literature Society Newsletter*, edited by Deshae Lott. (Savannah, GA: Department of Liberal Arts, Savannah State University, Spring 2007).
4. Nancy Genevieve, "A Kiss" In *NYX: Mother of Light*. (NOX Press, 2001); and ELM. Vol. 5, No. 2. Spring 1997.
5. Nancy Genevieve, "The Pond" and "Cicadas," *NYX: Daughter of Chaos*. (NOX Press, 2002).
6. "English Language Arts Standards » Anchor Standards » College and Career Readiness Anchor Standards for Language," *Common Core State Standards Initiative*. 2011.
7. From Chapter 17 of *The Adventures of Huckleberry Finn* by Mark Twain.

Chapter 6

Versing Life Together

Robert, Bobby, Bob
Fast, fleet, flown
Baby, boy, grown

— Anna Roseboro, "Our Son"

Even if your students are on board and initially excited about reading and talking about poetry, you may soon face a roadblock when you ask them to write it. Why? Perhaps it is because reading poetry can be such a challenging experience. Students may not think they are "deep" enough to write poetry. True, some students are naturally talented poets, but others learn by seeing how others write, being inspired by what they learn or simply by patterning the work of others. This probably is the best reason to read and study a variety of poetry before assigning all your students to write it. Once they understand the unique characteristics of poetry and experience the joy of word play by others, they eagerly accept the challenge to try versing, writing poems, and plays of their own.

Like many English teachers, you probably have been reading poems and having students write poetry as part of other lessons already. You may have had students write poems in response to literature as recommended when reading novels. You understand what a fine vehicle poetry is for showcasing young writers' understanding of literature and its connection to their lives. Now, in this chapter, notice that the purpose of writing poetry is different. It is for your students to experiment and conscientiously apply some of the elements of poetry to recreate experiences of their own, while meeting the curriculum and English language arts standards that ask students to demonstrate anchor tasks like

- producing clear and coherent writing in which the development, organization, and style are appropriate to task, purpose, and audience.
- developing and strengthening writing as needed by planning, revising, editing, rewriting, or trying a new approach.
- using technology, including the Internet, to produce and publish writing and to interact and collaborate with others.[1]

This chapter takes you and your students traveling into interesting side paths and offers suggestions for trying out different approaches to writing poetry. So feel free to let students get off the tour bus for a while and play with language. Invite them to splash around in fresh water streams, to wallow around in the mud a bit—manipulating words, forms, and imagery; to wander through the open markets checking out the collections you gathered to show how published writers craft their poems, sampling the goods, trying on styles; to experiment a bit, tasting different cuisines—all before you begin evaluating the quality of your students' writing.

Choose from the following activities, those in your own textbooks, or those you have found useful in the past. They all are designed to help your students compose a variety of poems that reflect their own personal experiences and observations, and encourage these burgeoning writers to dig deeper into quality published literature.

PATTERNING AND EMULATING

Want a compelling way for your reluctant writers to jump into poetry writing? Imitation. Modeling what others write. This is nothing new. Patterning and copying the work of others are traditional ways to learn difficult skills. Consider the painter and musician, the dancer and athlete. In each case, novices try to duplicate the strokes and colors, sound and technique, and form and movement of the masters. You can give your students similar opportunities during this poetry unit.

Lead the way and model for them. First—choose a poem that you love and, with your curious students watching, show how you work through the process of figuring out the pattern, then imitating that pattern. Ask them to look for rhyme and rhythm; draw their attention to sentence structure; entice them to imitate the kind of imagery; or challenge them to recreate the emotional impact through sounds and choice of words.

Perhaps you already are familiar with the poem, "Where I'm From" by George Ella Lyon or "The Delight Song of Tsoai-Talee" by Scott Momaday.

Use poems like these verses to begin, and then let the students pick one or two of their favorite poems from books on hand or online, and write a poem that emulates the structure, style, techniques, and rhythm of their chosen poem. See the companion website for this book for specific assignment handouts.

Structured poems may be your choice to introduce this kind of poetry writing. Limerick, haiku, and sonnet are traditional patterns of poetry—each with a specific rhyme or rhythm pattern. Trigger their memory with these patterns from elementary school.

Limerick: A five-line poem, usually funny, that follows an AABBA rhyme structure.

> There was an Old Man in a tree,
> Who was horribly bored by a Bee;
> When they said, 'Does it buzz?'
> He replied, 'Yes, it does!'
> 'It's a regular brute of a Bee!'
>
> —Edward Lear

How about having your music lovers pattern song lyrics? You may find useful ideas from M.U.S.I.C.—Musicians United for Songs in the Classroom, Inc. *Learning from Lyrics* website.

While you definitely want to spend some time modeling the different poems with or for your students, save plenty of time for them to experiment independently. Remember, your goal is to provide the classroom structure and cultivate a nurturing environment that makes for a safe and relaxed setting in which to experiment. Slowly but steadily release some of that control as the students become comfortable with the classroom routines.

The way you spend time shows what is important. During this portion of the unit, play and practice are important. Soon you can persuade them to perform for their peers either poetry by published poets or even poetry they write themselves. And just as athletes and dancers who practice a lot feel more confident performing, your maturing teens feel more self-assured when they have practiced.

Pantoums

One pattern that yields successful poems is a version of the less-familiar pantoum, a poem consisting of eight lines – each is used twice. A pantoum is less intimidating for reluctant poets because it is based more on repetition than on rhyme or rhythm patterns. A pantoum can be used as an alternative book report to capture key events, a memorable scene, or a favorite character from a literary work or from a life experience. Here is a sample poem written when Anne Brown's seventh-grade class finished reading *Brown Girl Dreaming* by Jacqueline Woodson, an autobiographical book written primarily in free verse.

Begin by writing four original lines:

(1) A girl named Jackie
(2) In a country divided by race
(3) Moved from North to South
(4) Living with the blanket of her grandparents love

Repeat lines two and four, and add lines five and six to expand ideas introduced in lines two and four, like this:

(2) In a country divided by race
(5) Two siblings and one parent in a long ride "home"
(4) Living with the blanket of her grandparents love
(6) Buried five days a week giving witness to Jehovah

Repeat lines five and six, and add lines seven and eight to expand ideas mentioned in lines five and six, like this:

(5) Two siblings and a parent in a long ride "home"
(7) Anchored in childhood by candy on Friday and ribbons on Sunday
(6) Buried five days a week giving witness to Jehovah
(8) Moving again, New York City, new sibling, new life

Finally, repeat lines one, three, seven and eight in this order:

(7) Anchored in childhood by candy on Friday and ribbons on Sunday
(3) Moved from North to South
(8) Moving again, New York City, new sibling, new life
(1) A girl named Jackie

The result is a lovely poem that captures the essence of the story. As you read and then write your own sample of this pattern poem, you can see how much grammar, usage, and punctuation students must employ to make sure pronouns are the right number and gender and that the verbs are the right tense to make sense as they add more lines! You can bet Ms. Brown had her students do just that when they looked back and saw some of the issues they missed when they were drafting.

After sharing this sample pantoum or one you compose yourself, your students are likely to be inspired to write their own.

Lazy Sonnets

Here (see figure 6.1) is a simple structured format that works well with ninth-grade students and gutsy younger ones. You may assign these "lazy sonnets" after a formal study of poetry that includes lessons on the traditional fourteen-line sonnets, after teaching Shakespeare's *Romeo and Juliet* or another play that includes sonnets. The students use this exercise to practice poetry and also to summarize their thoughts about the play. The only rules are to use fourteen words and to follow the rhyme pattern of an Elizabethan (Shakespearean) or Italian (Petrarchan) sonnet.

As a culminating activity following a study of a text, invite students to simply encapsulate a key idea, show the characters, conflicts, or a theme of the fiction or nonfiction piece; to use just fourteen words and end with a rhymed couplet. You could divide the class into five groups, one per act, or a number that fits the play you are studying, and then have students in each group write about their assigned act. On the left is a lazy sonnet Kaveh wrote based on Act V of *Romeo and Juliet*. On the right is a lazy sonnet written in Nancy Himel's class when studying, "The Rime of the Ancient Mariner" by Samuel Taylor Coleridge.

What is particularly fun about writing these lazy sonnets is that they are manageable for a range of students. Students who are frustrated by writing other poetry likely can compose a lazy sonnet successfully. Some even include a rhyme or rhythm pattern as well as the couplet! Your creative students may write quickly enough to enter their sonnets on the computer

TEXTBOX 6.1: LAZY SONNETS

Romeo and Juliet, Act V	"The Rime of the Ancient Mariner"
Paris slain by Romeo.	Mariner shoots. Albatross dies.
Romeo then slew himself.	Storms blow. Crew dies.
Later Juliet slew herself.	Mariner prays. Penance granted:
Madness Sadness	Hoary story.

and print out these unrevised sonnets by the end of the period. Quick. Fun. Enlightening for students. Revealing to you.

CAPTURING PERSONAL EXPERIENCES IN POETRY AND DRAMA

Much writing is autobiographical, portraying personal experiences. But it can be more. Joseph Epstein writes, "The personal essay is, in my experience, a form of discovery." What one discovers in writing such essays is where one stands on complex issues, problems, questions, and subjects. In writing the essay, one tests one's feelings, instincts, and thoughts in the crucible of composition.[2] This self-discovery is also true when writing poetry.

For their poetry assignments encourage but do not require that students use their personal experiences and observations as they imitate the structure and pattern of published poetry they enjoy. In keeping with the philosophy of the National Writing Project, write along with your students. This keeps you attuned to what it feels like to write "on demand" and also gives you an opportunity to reveal to your students a little of who you are when you are not teaching. The poem opening this chapter is one written about my son's growing up and leaving home.

Initially, you may be uncomfortable writing about your personal experiences along with your young teenagers, but it is well worth any risk of discomfort. Be prepared; you and your students may be surprised by what comes out in this kind of writing. Occasionally, however, several of you may decide not to show it to anyone or read it aloud. Honor these decisions. You can decline to share; let them decline, too.

GRADING STUDENT'S ORIGINAL POETRY

What works well is to customize a rubric you've used in the past that outlines the knowledge and skills you are measuring. Is their ability to write an original poem based on

- length?
- use of specific kinds or number of poetic devices?
- a specific rhyme or rhythm pattern?
- fresh use of language: vivid verbs? concrete nouns?
- words chosen for the sound and expressive power?
- matching the pattern of a published poem?

Decide what a complete poem will be in terms of such features as those mentioned earlier. What would a student need to demonstrate to earn a C? a B? an A?

Consider:

- C = poem meets minimum length requirement and has three of five suggested poetic devices to recreate an experience or observation
- B = poem meets minimum length requirement, has all five suggested poetic devices, and has words that suggest an identifiable tone of the poet about the experience or observation
- A = poem exceeds minimum length requirement, has all five suggested poetic devices used in fresh and creative ways, reflects words that suggest an identifiable tone of the poet, and has active verbs and concrete nouns that clearly and cleverly recreate an identifiable experience or observation.

Then ask students to write a note to explain how their original poem fits the definition of poetry given earlier. (See chapter 5.)

WRITING ABOUT POETRY

Responding to poetry through essay writing is an important component of poetry study. You can combine writing poetry and writing about poetry in the same unit. If so, it would be beneficial to begin with a quick review of Poetry T.I.M.E. as suggested in the previous chapter. Then select and project on screen an appropriately challenging poem and have the students conduct a T.I.M.E. analysis of it. Projecting the poem can be better for whole class work because all must focus their attention up front. See chapter 5 "Taking T.I.M.E. to Teach Poetry" for steps for multiple readings.

If you provide students copies of the poem, also give them a couple of colored pencils. In this case, you have the students underline what strikes them as they read the poem to themselves. On the first reading, encourage the students to underline appealing or thought-provoking words and phrases. Then before the second reading, ask them to exchange pencils for another color and mark what attracts them on this second reading. It is fine to underline the same word or phrase in a second color. Then conclude this version of multiple readings by asking students to read aloud the word phrases they have underlined. If one student reads a line first, it is all right for another student to repeat it. It is likely that the repeated words and phrases reveal the theme or main ideas of the poem.

Next, after whatever opening reading strategy you choose, have students complete their T.I.M.E. worksheets on their own, answering questions about the title, thoughts, and theme; imagery; music; and emotion. Then have them turn and talk about their observations with a partner, using their six-inch voices. Finally, conduct a full-class discussion of student reactions and responses. Remind them to use the P.I.E. format—oral practice for writing an analysis of the poem. Ask them to state their point/observation about the poem, illustrate that observation with a direct quotation from the poem, and explain the significance of that illustration.

In-Class Writing about Poetry: Telling the T.I.M.E.

Carefully read the assigned poem noting the structure, imagery, and meaning or message for you. Then write a complete essay in response to the poem that includes the following:

- Summary of the poem—What is it about?
- Structure of the poem—What poetic devices does the poet use?
- Personal Response to the poem—What poetic devices help create this personal response?
- A thesis statement that indicates the kind of poem it is and your personal response to it.
- A body that explains ways the structure of the poem influences your response.
- Quotations that support your observations.

You may write on the poem and use the space below it for your notes.

For homework or during the next class meeting, assign a three-part essay in which they write the analysis of that poem or one of their own choosing. They should use the information they gathered while "telling the T.I.M.E." of the poem. See textbox 5.1 for alternative approach.

Assigning the Poetry Project or Notebook

An effective way to reinforce the interests raised and skills developed during a poetry unit is to have the students assemble a poetry notebook. The collection should include poems students have read and enjoyed, as well as poems they have written themselves. Decide how much time you can devote to this project and select activities that may be organized around one or more of the following topics:

- Poems by a single poet
- Poems written on a single theme (love, family, hobby, seasons, etc.)
- Poems employing common poetic devices
- Poems reflecting a specific culture or nationality

It is imperative to inform your students at the beginning of the poetry unit what they are to assemble for this poetry notebook. In this way, they can think about and collect poems throughout the weeks you spend on formal poetry study. Encourage students to use available digital devices and computers to search for, write, and save their poems. Some students may decide to expand their poetry notebooks with original drawings, video, photo, or audio components that can be shared live or online. Remind them to keep a record of their sources including URL addresses and dates viewed.

Assigning a poetry project is a good way to incorporate a research component into your instruction, too. Your school librarian can help students find background and biographical information on their selected poet and, if access to the Internet is available, refer students to preselected, age-appropriate websites. Your students may prefer to create an electronic version of this notebook and post it for sharing with other students in like courses around the country and around the world.

In planning for this project, check online sites with safe environments for students to post their writing. Some teachers you know may have produced class anthologies using www.lulu.com, a free site for composing. It includes, for a modest fee, an option to print booklets that others can purchase. Some sites require parent permission to post online.

The choices students have to make for this project—conducting research, writing and selecting poems, deciding formats, creating order, using technology, collaborating with classmates—all are part of an authentic assessment

Students using tablets: Exchange poetry across the country by Internet

where students are showing what they know and are able to do based on skills they bring and those they learn under your carefully designed tutelage.

WRITING A ONE-ACT PLAY

After studying a play, you may assign students to write one of their own and wonder where to begin. Remind them that one of the key features of drama is dialogue that reveals character and advances plot. Your students probably will be most challenged by what to have the actors do while they are speaking. Cresence Birder, a teacher of ninth-grade students, addressed this with diagrams. See the companion website for "Writing a One-Act Play." She found that some students visualize better when they draw a diagram of the set, or create charts with arrows, boxes, and circles. Periodically, invite your students to share with their classmates the strategies they devise to help make sense of the text. Shared peer perceptions increase peer comprehension.

Ms. Birder reflected, "One student even commented, 'Blocking the scenes in our plays helped me envision each scene. This enabled me to find ways of producing more action in the play.' For many students, including this type of activity in the brainstorming process dynamically shaped the idea of the plot in their heads to fit the stage; drawing some of the more significant moments of blocking helped to reveal what ideas were most realistic and doable in a theater space, and which ideas would be far-fetched or perhaps better suited for film. Also, this assignment provided students with an opportunity to process their thoughts visually." This strategy may work for you, too.

RECITING POETRY OUT LOUD AND IN CHORAL FORM

Invite local poets to come read or perform for your students and include time in class for students to prepare and perform poetry for one another. This can be a powerful experience for speakers and listeners as evidenced by the opening poem to chapter 5, "Words, Words, Words"; it is a poetic response to a performance of student poets. Consider, too, some of the online sites that show poets reading and performing their own work.

When teaching *Romeo and Juliet*, for example, you could require that students memorize the prologue to Act One, or choose a short twelve- to fourteen-line poem that fits a topic of study in your curriculum. To aid students in learning the lines, on the day you introduce the play or unit, perform the poem yourself, and then have the students echo it back to you, line by line. On subsequent days, begin the period with the class standing and reciting the poem together. Since the poem previews the plot of the play or theme of unit, this oral, auditory activity can be a regular reminder of what happens as the drama unfolds or the topic is explored.

Another idea is to assign a dramatic poem and have small groups develop their version of a choral reading to perform for the class. A classic performance piece is "The Highwayman" by Alfred Noyes. For a chilling end, suggest the closing line be spoken by a single, soft-voiced student. If students prefer a rap poem, remind them to articulate clearly and not get lost in the rhythm beats.

A powerful poem is Maya Angelou's "On the Pulse of Morning," which she recited at the Presidential Inauguration Ceremony for Bill Clinton in 1993. Not surprising, no two groups may develop the same script. That is just fine. Seeing and hearing different "versions" of this poem expands the students' understanding of and appreciation for the ideas, sounds, and images of diverse groups of people Angelou mentions in her memorable masterpiece.

Your teaching colleagues may even welcome an opportunity to have their students witness poetry out loud. On performance day, have each class decide the group that gives the most powerful or interesting performance, and then commission this group to represent the class and go "on the road" to recite their rendition of the poem to other classes that meet in your hallway. What pride students feel performing poetry for other students!

CELEBRATING POETRY

By this time, you and your students have read, written, and performed poetry in class; you are ready for a special poetry celebration. It can be simply a special time during the regular class period or a bigger event to which family and friends are invited to meet in the cafeteria, auditorium, or library.

For the celebration, invite all the students to memorize and perform a selected poem—one that they have read or one that they have written. If you have multiple classes celebrating together, you could hold an "open mike" time where volunteers come forward to perform their chosen poem. To assure that someone "volunteers," ask students to sign up ahead of time. On Celebration Day

- have students display their notebooks laid on tables like a science fair exhibition,
- invite guests to leave post-it notes with commendations on poems they like,
- have one student master or mistress of ceremonies who welcomes the guests,
- have a second master or mistress of ceremonies who calls on the volunteers to recite their poems, and
- invite everyone in attendance to share the light refreshments.

Be prepared for on-the-spot volunteers who see the joy of performing and want to share the spotlight.

All of this means planning well ahead to reserve the space, invite administrators to attend, have microphones in place, and refreshments bought or brought and laid out. Students should be recruited to help set up and clean up.

If you work together with other teachers, you may be able turn this into a school-wide event. Post student poetry in the halls. Write it with colored chalk on the sidewalks (with permission of the principal, of course). Encourage the students to enter their writing in local, state, and national poetry contests in print, audiovisual, or digital formats, or perform in age-appropriate poetry slam venues.

This Poetry Celebration is the perfect time to invite students to recite poetry of their nationality, culture, or home language. Since poetry is written to be heard, it does not matter whether everyone in the audience understands every spoken word. Just invite these students to recite a favorite poem and let them bask in the pleasure of sharing themselves in a language close to their hearts. To enhance the experience of the listeners, encourage those students who are comfortable reciting the poem in a language other than English to first give a brief synopsis of the poem.

CONNECTING BEYOND THE CLASSROOM

Many educator websites provide online opportunities for students to expand their knowledge of topics addressed in the books used in language arts courses across North America.

A PERSONAL STORY

When I lived in California and attended a national convention for English teachers, I met one from Florida. We set up a "Coast to Coast" project in which students wrote to each other about the poetry that both classes were studying. We teachers posted selected works by a poet from our own state and invited students to discuss their responses online. The resulting conversation offered them insightful peer perspectives while affirming that students on both coasts have to learn and apply the same kinds of analytical and evaluative skills during their study of poetry.

CONCLUSION

Poetry writing need not lead to student defeat or frustration, sending your school year tour bus into a ditch. Your creative, well-structured lesson planning and nurturing instruction can create an environment in which students compose and recite poetry with pleasure and poise, with personality and pride. Their original poems are likely to become valued souvenirs of this portion of the trip. You can confirm the fine work of your students and encourage them to submit their poetry for publication in print or on safe Internet sites. Of course, support students who decide to enter local poetry slams and attend them if you can.

Celebrate poetry with your students and watch how what they learn about the power of careful word choices, deliberate crafting, attention to organization, and impact of appearance carries over into their reading and writing other fiction and nonfiction. With your help, providing them with a key to unlock the poetry of others and to release poetic endowments of their own, your students look forward to "versing" their lives in poetry, the way I learned to turn my prose thoughts about my son, Robert, into the verse that opens this chapter.

NOTES

1. *Common Core Standards*, 2011.
2. Joseph Epstein, "The Personal Essay: A Form of Discovery." In *The Norton Book of Personal Essays*, edited by Joseph Epstein. (New York: W. W. Norton and Company. 1997), 15.

Chapter 7

Learning to Speak Publicly

It is no longer an advantage to speak English, but a requirement! Just speaking English isn't so impressive anymore—unless you speak it really well.[1]

—Heather Hansen

Are you one of the English teachers who bemoan the fact that you find it challenging to teach students to give a "good" speech? Like colleagues in your department, do you acknowledge that students do well on "oral reports," yet something still is lacking? Speech-giving really is different from giving an oral report. But how?

Pose a few questions, and the features become clear. Start your unit on public speaking asking students what they notice about a good speaker. Surprisingly, they seldom comment on the content of the speech, but instead point out aspects of delivery like giving verbal clues to organization pattern, making eye contact, using gestures, rate of speaking, clear articulation, varied intonation, poise, and even attire. Of course, middle school students probably do not use these terms, but what they mention shows clearly that how the report is delivered is the key feature that makes the speech effective.

If you expect your students to become successful, competent, and confident speakers, it seems only right that you incorporate into your lesson-planning opportunities for students to observe and critique good speaking and also time to write and practice their own speeches. Ask them to watch television news reporters. Find and show them short video clips of men and women in politics and business delivering speeches. Watch an inspirational speaker giving a talk. Websites such as TED Talks include presentations on a range of topics by an even wider range of speakers. With careful screening, you will find video appropriate and inspiring for use in your classroom. Showing them speeches on culturally relevant topics will surely increase students' eagerness to improve their own skills.

Urge your students to watch their teachers. Encourage them to pay attention to the delivery styles of their imams, pastors, priests, and rabbis. After just a few observations, your teen monitors can assemble a list of those characteristics of content, structure, style, and vocal qualities that make oral presentations simple to follow and easy to remember. Next, encourage students to pattern effective deliveries that fit their own personal style.

WRITING FOR SPEAKING

Giving a speech is more than reading an essay aloud. A successful speech is both an oral and visual presentation designed for a specific audience, place, and purpose. Since public speaking is designed to be heard, few listeners come prepared to take notes. Writing with that understanding in mind will ensure that the audience will retain more of what they hear if the content and delivery are designed to help listeners know what to listen for and provide spoken cues to remind listeners of what they have heard. Another significant difference in writing for speaking and writing for reading is that oral presentations include spoken citations. Furthermore, conscientious speakers dress for the occasion, and they use voice inflections, physical gestures, and movement to enhance what is being said.

By spring of the school year, your students are becoming comfortable enough with you and their classmates to give oral presentations with more assurance than in the opening semester. Spring also is a good time to write and then deliver more formal informative or persuasive speeches, written to be evaluated for qualities of delivery. Speech writing is another opportunity to hone their research, writing, and speaking skills for authentic audiences and meet those curriculum standards for oral presentations.

You can help your students understand the value of writing good speeches by telling them that top-ranking leaders hire professional speech writers because it is vital to their success to be effective, inspiring presenters. It is not that these men and women are not smart; it is because they know writing speeches is different from writing reports. As with other kinds of writing, having your students read written samples and view delivered speeches can help them see the differences.

Looking closely at written speeches, students will notice several distinct features. They will see that speech writers use more repetition to guide audience in following, comprehending, and recalling ideas presented. Close reading will reveal the use of shorter, more declarative sentences consisting of vivid verbs, concrete nouns, graphic images, and, like poetry, vocabulary chosen for its sound and suggestive power. As students will have discovered in your lessons on text structures, they will see written speeches incorporate carefully chosen transitions and signal words. They are used to hold the speech together while keeping the listeners on track with the positions, arguments, and stories being presented in informative, persuasive, as well as entertaining speeches.

BRIDGING THE GAP BETWEEN READING AND WRITING A SPEECH

A smooth segue between showing the text of a speech and writing a speech is presenting a sample speech yourself or a video of a speech being delivered. Draw their attention to the features of an effective oral presentation and that speeches are both aural and visual. The audience pays attention to what the speaker says and how he or she looks and uses the physical space and supportive or distracting gestures.

Choose and show a couple of the TED Talks on topics your class has been studying. This time, turn off the volume and ask the students to simply watch the speaker. How is he or she using the physical space? What gestures seem natural without being distracting? Then turn the volume up and ask students to pay attention to vocal qualities. How does the speaker pace his or her presentation? Use pauses? Modulate his or her voice? Articulate words?

Remind your students to be thoughtful speakers who take into consideration what the audience sees as it listens. This begins with attire, gestures, and use of physical space. Most important, speakers also practice ahead of time, develop poise, and are able to deliver their speeches at a pace that is easy to follow. They use pauses, pacing, and volume to attract and retain attention throughout the speech.

Applying Known Persuasive Strategies

If you decide to have your students write the text of a persuasive speech, spend a little time talking about persuasive strategies, organizational patterns, and ways of determining what the audience thinks and believes before trying to convince them to change. Refer them to lessons learned reading and writing persuasive essays and articles, noting how most writers appealed to the head, the heart, and the pocket of their audiences.

SPEAKING FOR DIFFERENT PURPOSES

Generally, there are four basic kinds of speeches. During the course of a school year, you can ask students to prepare and present one of each: to

Presenting together can reduce angst

inform, to persuade, to entertain, and to commemorate. You do not have to wait until later in the school year to have a formal speech unit of two or three weeks, assignments for analysis of speeches, and the time for them to complete their presentation. While elements of preparation and practice both are keys to effective public presentations, having given oral presentations throughout the year students have personal experience to reflect upon if your curriculum requires direct instruction on public speaking.

The informative speech could be on what students learn about the author of a book. A persuasive speech can be preparation for a service club speech contests like those of the Rotary and Optimists Club, or simply to convince their classmates to read a particular book.

To help students relax, give them the option to present the speech in the persona of a character from a piece of literature you read together as a class. In fact, the persuasive speech assignment could be to persuade a character in one of the short stories to read an independently chosen book the student has just finished! The speech to commemorate could be one honoring a special friend, family member, community leader, person in history, or literary character. These commemorative speeches could be solemn and serious or entertaining and humorous, but always in good taste.

PICKING A TOPIC AND PLANNING A SPEECH

For older students, you may design a news-related speech assignment where students are expected to think critically about authentic purposes for persuasive speaking. They conduct research, use correct citation and documentation, and then write and present a speech on a current issue. In this case, too, you can link the assignment to a piece of literature you are studying. You could ask students to select a news-related topic that might interest one of the characters from a novel or article the class has read. Or they could write a speech to address a problem in the school or community, and when possible record and send the speech to the group that could or should be addressing that problem. Authentic reasons to communicate well will inspire your students to do just that.

Constructing the Speech

Vital to your planning is allotting time for students to construct the speech and practice it. Your future orators soon recognize that writing to speak is very different from simply writing an essay and reading it aloud. They realize that shorter, less complex sentences make for better speaking. They see they need to state the goal or position, illustrate with example, explain it, and review it in much the way they used P.I.E. patterns in class discussion. As speakers, they are responsible not only for letting their audience know what the speech is about using some kind of verbalized sign post but also for providing transitions to help listeners process the information and stay on track.

Your particularly astute students may recall and apply what they learned in the poetry unit about choosing and arranging words based on their sound and suggestive power. You can further reduce anxiety by sharing with your prospective orators these self-check questions about introducing their speeches, as well as providing various kinds of explanation and supporting evidence that lead to more successful speeches.

Getting Off to a Good Start and Using a Variety of Evidence—Self-Check

Do I provide adequate support for each main section of my speech? (Check the number of times you include each of these supporting materials in your speech.)

_____ illustrations/examples   _____ explanations
_____ definitions   _____ restatements

	statistics/numbers		humor
	comparison/contrast		opinion of experts
	testimony		quotations

Having students make a script of their speech is a practical way to have them practice the grammar they have been learning, too. Their goal is to communicate clearly both in writing and in speaking in an appropriate grammar, Standard English, or otherwise. Their choice of grammar makes the difference in how well they get their ideas across to their audience even if their purpose is to entertain peers in their class commemorating a character in a story, a historical figure in history, a real friend, or family member.

Practicing, Practicing, Practicing

Insist that your students get feedback on their speeches before presenting them in class for evaluation. This listener could be a friend or family member, or if that is not reasonable to expect in the setting where you teach, this someone could be a classmate. Practicing aloud is the only way for students to know for certain they are familiar enough with their speech's content to deliver it with confidence, making eye contact, using gestures, pronouncing words correctly and clearly, varying the pace of the speaking, and maintaining their poise.

SPEECH PEER-EVALUATION FORM

Here are speech features students can focus on during practice and you can measure during assessment. Adapt this one based on an assignment topic called, "Optimism Is the Right Stuff."

Speech Writer: _____

Period: _____

Topic: _____

_____

Use a scale of 1–5 (low–high) to indicate how close the speaker has come to meeting the goal of writing an interesting, effective, believable, and winning speech?

Introduction: Opening grabs and holds attention by using

_____ Startling statistics?

_____ Heartwarming, heart-wrenching story?

_____ Amusing anecdote (story that illustrates problem)?

Body Organization Plan—Describes *problem* with details from research and answers the following questions:

_____ Who is affected, concerned, involved?
_____ What is the nature, significance of problem?
_____ When did it become a problem? How long? Into future?
_____ Where is problem experienced? Where are solutions planned?
_____ Why should audience be concerned?
_____ How is or how can the problem be solved?
_____ Each paragraph develops/explains main idea.

Conclusion Technique—Shows how optimism has helped cope with the problem or gives reasons for optimism.

Dressing for the Occasion

Students sometimes wonder what they should be paying attention to when they practice a speech. Share guidelines to assure these soon-to-be public speakers that they are on the right track. Strongly suggest that they time themselves as they give their speech at least three times standing in front of a mirror, holding their notes on the same index cards they plan to use when they give their speech in public. If they can look up at themselves and keep talking through their speech, they probably are prepared to look up and make more frequent eye contact with their audience.

Encourage your students wear something special on the day they give the speech, an outfit that is especially neat, comfortable, and appropriate for their intended audience. Choosing what to wear reminds them that people in an audience are spectators influenced by the speaker's physical appearance and posture. If it is appropriate at your school, have on hand a suit coat or tie your male students can borrow on speech day. Females should avoid dingle-dangle earrings that distract from their message when speakers move their heads. When resources are available at home or at school, recommend that your students make an audio or video recording and listen and watch to hear and see what others will experience when the students deliver their speeches.

Providing students with probing questions helps them evaluate their speech plans and encourages them to modify them before presenting to the public. For example, if you assign a speech to persuade, ask students to include arguments that appeal to the head, the heart, and the pocket:

• Does this speech make appeals to the *head* (definitions, statistics, explanations, and comparison/contrast)?

- Does this speech make appeals to the *heart* (humor, explanation, illustrations, quotations, testimony or stories about real people)?
- Does this speech make appeals to the *pocket* (definitions, facts, statistics, and comparison/contrast related to money)?

Students who are asked to give a little more attention to observing; assigned to point out the qualities of a good speech; and given time to research, write, and practice, become attuned to differences in effectiveness. These young communicators no longer are content simply to give a report but will endeavor to present a speech.

LISTENING TO AND GRADING SPEECHES

Consider the two sides of communication—the SPEAKER and the LISTENER—as you continue massaging your speech assignments and scheduling their presentation.

Because critical listening and useful commenting are skills of equal value to speaking well, include opportunities for students to provide written feedback to each speaker. To make it more efficient, consider a five-day cycle with each student required to sign up to speak on a date he or she prefers and to provide specific feedback for classmates' speeches on the days he or she does not speak. See table 7.1 to help organize and have a productive week of speaking and listening.

Have them use the same feedback chart you use for grading and have each student focus on just one feature each of the four days in the cycle. Collect feedback sheets, review, staple together those for each speaker, and return them to each one at the end of the round of speeches.

As an additional incentive to prepare and present well, you could ask students to do three things on the day they present their speech in class.

- By midnight of the day before they give their speech in class, submit their written outline of the speech to your online class folder or send to you by e-mail.
- On the day of their speech, sign up on the board indicating the speaking order they prefer. (usually one to five). Some students like to speak and get it over; others like to observe what others do before they speak. Usually, five or six speeches per day are enough.
- By midnight the day they give their speech in class, submit a self-evaluation along with the letter grade they believe they earned on that speech. If their grade is the same as yours, raise their grade 1/2 step. C+ becomes B−; B− becomes B; B+ becomes A−, and so forth.

DAY	RED	GREEN	PURPLE	ORANGE	BLUE
1	SPEAKING (NO FEEDBACK)	Comment on CONTENT (Appropriate for audience, variety of support, appeals, quality of evidence and resources, sources cited, etc.)	Comment on ORGANIZATION (Introduction with SIGN POST (statement of purpose)) TRANSITIONS (appropriate for kind of speech) CONCLUSION (summary, reflection, or projection without introducing new ideas)	Comment on VOCAL ISSUES (Articulation, intonation, pace, pauses, volume, etc.)	Comment on APPEARANCE (Appropriate gestures, use of physical space, visual aids, etc.)
2	APPEARANCE	SPEAKING	CONTENT	ORGANIZATION	VOCAL ISSUES
3	VOCAL ISSUES	APPEARANCE	SPEAKING	CONTENT	ORGANIZATION
4	ORGANIZATION	VOCAL ISSUES	APPEARANCE	SPEAKING	CONTENT
5	CONTENT	ORGANIZATION	VOCAL ISSUES	APPEARANCE	SPEAKING

Table 7.1. Organize a week of speeches with color teams

Resist both looking at their self-evaluation or grade until after you complete the grading, and lowering their grade if theirs is lower than yours.

A portion of each prepared speech grade can be

- 20 % —On-time submission of speech outline or draft in class
- 15 % —Feedback on drafts of classmate's speech
- 30 % —FINAL draft or outline of own speech
- 30 % —Presentation of own speech
- 5 % —On-time submission of self-evaluation

Because most English language arts standards tend to equate speaking and listening and require students to show growth in both, taking a full week for presenting speeches seems to be good use of time.

CONCLUSION

Proficiency in speaking well is the ticket to career advancement in many professions. For this reason, educators have the responsibility to help students acquire this knowledge as part of their classroom experience. You can help them expand their knowledge and skills by incorporating regular opportunities to learn and use rhetorical skills ethically. Asking students to pay attention to effective writers and speakers raises their awareness about ways people judge others. This is based on their skill using appropriate language in specific settings, presenting themselves with confidence and competence. If they have had practice delivering informal and formal speeches, they can access these skills when they want to be perceived positively by those they wish to impress with their improving education.

NOTE

1. Heather Hansen, "Speak English Clearly and Grammatically, and Boost your Success!" Articles Base, n.d. http://leadershiptrainingtutorials.com/leadershiptraining/uncategorized/speak-english-clearly-and-grammatically-and-boost-your-success/#.W4AnyOhKhAE (accessed August 24, 2018).

Chapter 8

Teaching Standard English Grammar and Terms in Media Arts

The mark of an effective speaker is the ability to adapt to a variety of audiences and settings and to perform appropriately in diverse social situations.[1]

—Clella Jaffe

A dear friend is an accomplished welder and a talented musician who can skillfully navigate a luxury tour bus through dense urban traffic and parallel park it with only inches to spare. And she is pathological about talking in public, except in casual conversation; she believes people judge her intellect by her speech. Given her accented regional dialect and limited experience reading and writing Standard English, she doesn't want to appear ignorant, so she self-muzzles. She seldom writes anything formal and only writes an informal note in an emergency, and seldom communicates online, believing people judge her education by her writing. So, she corrals her speaking and curbs her writing, keeping herself to herself.

True, my friend left school early, married young, and soon became the sole wage earner for her family of three children. Even though she is gifted mentally and manually, she still feels hampered, unable to advance on any of her career paths primarily because she lacks proficiency communicating in Standard English. So sad. So frustrating.

This story illustrates just one of the reasons for this chapter. How one speaks, writes, and uses technology matters. The ideas that follow can help you fulfill the charge, meet the obligation, and ensure that the students you teach do not have to live like this, stifling their thoughts because they are ashamed of their oral and written skills, or their ability to navigate using current technologies as receivers or senders.

Teachers have to help students realize that their future success may be thwarted if they know and use only nonstandard grammar and avoid learning the grammar of the media. Share your own stories with those you teach and inspire them to take full advantage of the opportunities provided in school for them to read, hear, and speak Standard English; to write in a style or version of English appropriate for the setting; and to use current technology for researching for writing and communicating in a range of situations. Working toward the Common Core Anchor Standards for Language will help guide you and your students to achieving the goal of skillful communication.

WHY TEACH STANDARD ENGLISH

It is important, as early as middle school, to teach students the rules of Standard English and hold them accountable for following the rules in many settings that can be beneficial to them. They should know that in the national and international communities, English is the language of commerce, technology, and diplomacy. You can substantiate these claims by showing them "An English Speaking World," part of the video series, *The Story of English*. Hearing from others in a resource such as this, narrated by respected former PBS journalist Robert McNeil, not only can help your students understand the

Grammar taught in context works

history and development of the English language but also can convince them of the value of knowing how to write and speak English well.

Your students, like most humans, yearn to be understood and respected for their mental acumen, and you can build on this basic desire. Design classroom activities to review and teach the basics of English grammar, plan writing workshops in which students hear comments on the effectiveness of their writing, and structure guided discussions in which students receive feedback on their oral presentations. These lessons raise their awareness, demonstrate the impact of their choices, and help them see that using nonstandard grammar can obscure their own written and oral communication and that using Standard English grammar can clarify both. The challenge for you is to honor their home language and, at the same time, give them the knowledge necessary to code-switch or blend dialects when a situation deems it appropriate.

INSTRUCTING IN OR OUT OF CONTEXT: FORMAL OR INFORMAL LESSONS

By the end of middle school, teachers expect students to be familiar with parts of speech, parts of a sentence, and with verbals. They also expect students to write using consistent agreement between subject and verb, pronouns and their antecedents. Most curricula for the later grades include lessons on a range of sentence structures, various sentence starters, and appropriate punctuation for these more complex sentences. Sometimes formal grammar lessons are taught, and students take tests on identifying grammatical structures and correcting errors in sentences or paragraphs. Other schools teach grammar entirely through student writing. In either setting, when a problem arises, you should teach the rule and give students exercises to practice applying it.

Both approaches to teaching grammar eventually work, but lasting learning seems to occur when you hold students responsible for correct grammar in their everyday writing and allot time for review and revision before grading for grammar. When they see it merely as a game of memorization or identification, students soon lose interest and seldom apply grammar rules beyond the classroom. Hold your students accountable and encourage them to become more astute speakers and writers.

After a concept is taught, add the correct use of that concept to the evaluation standards on subsequent graded writing assignments. Consider adapting rubrics from your text or those found online, like the Six Traits® rubric published by the Northwest Regional Educational Laboratory. Most published rubrics include grammar as one criterion for evaluating speaking and writing. Students can become more comfortable in formal and informal settings, in and out of school knowing when and how to use Standard English to achieve their own purposes.

SKETCHING TO CLARIFY THE
FUNCTION OF PARTS OF SPEECH

Even though many students study some grammar in elementary school, you still can start this direct instruction lesson by showing students the function of "parts" of speech in everyday conversations. This first example is to demonstrate that grammar is not just about rules, but about effective communication. You can show students what this looks like by using visual symbols to represent the shared understanding of ideas and images. If you were to visit a classroom to "see" and "hear" what this lesson would look and sound like on the opening day of direct instruction of formal grammar, like the paragraphs that follow, your notes may have recorded what happened in that particular teacher's classroom.

Draw a stick figure to represent the speaker; draw a second stick figure to represent the listener. Then draw balloons by the heads of each figure, with small bubbles connecting the balloons to each head. Try to draw, as exact as possible, the same image, say, of a bird flying over a bush, in both the speaker/writer's balloon and the listener/reader's balloon. The images are not precisely identical, but neither are shared messages. Explain that clear and

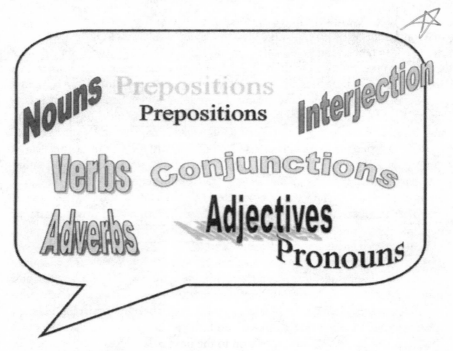

Figure 8.1.   Add each part of speech as you describe it

effective communication occurs when you can transmit your ideas effectively to your listener or reader.

Now sketch on the board another stick figure with a very large cartoon balloon that represents verbal communication—either written or spoken. Next, divide that balloon into eight segments to represent the eight common parts of speech. (See figure 8.1.)

Of course, there is no need to use the exact words you hear when you visit this imaginary classroom, but you may find this to be an effective way to review these basic parts of speech with your middle school students or new college students who may not have thought about grammar from this perspective. Write or draw while explaining why languages have different parts of speech. So, here goes!

"When we want to name people, places, things, events, and activities, we use nouns. A noun is one part of speech. Nouns name. When we want to talk about what those nouns do, we use verbs. They are another part of speech. Verbs can express action as well as indicate when the action takes place. There are other functions of verbs we'll talk about later.

"Now, occasionally, we want to clarify what the listener/reader imagines by modifying the mental image of a noun. Adjectives modify or limit nouns."

SHOWING HOW MODIFIERS FUNCTION

Continue in this fashion and give examples of ways that adjectives limit or modify nouns: "When I was eight years old, I got a ball for my birthday. On the opening page of the grammar section of your journal, draw the ball I received." Pause a moment. Invariably, the students draw different types and sizes of balls. Now add adjectives that limit the image of the noun by telling what kind (rubber), what size (little), and what color (purple with red diamonds around the circumference). By adding adjectives, thus creating a shared mental image, you communicate an image ever-closer to the ball received.

Reiterate this concept and use any noun that elicits a wide variety of images and enables you to limit the meaning of the noun simply by adding adjectives indicating kind, size, and color. Choose an example to fit your students' backgrounds. Consider the example of the dog, a horse, or a sweater. Begin saying just "dog." Let the students write the kind of dog they imagine. Then you add modifiers and ask how mental images come closer and closer to the dog you really received. Students begin to understand the value of linguistic precision.

Point back to the cartoon bubble depicting parts of speech, add the three you've described so far, and move on to the next part of speech, the modifier for verbs. Remind students that speakers and writers often want to limit or modify others' mental image of an action. In this case, the writer would use another part of speech, an adverb. Adverbs modify verbs by telling when, where, how, and to what extent. If students bring up the fact that adverbs also are used to answer these questions about adjectives or other adverbs, acknowledge this fact and move on.

In the presentation, you may illustrate your explanation with the verb "to walk" and then ask students to suggest adverbs that tell where the action could take place (outside, inside, around, out, etc.). Usually, they suggest prepositional phrases, too, like "around the corner" or "across the field." Tell them they are correct—sometimes phrases (or groups of words) can modify a noun or verb—and that you will talk about these kinds of modifiers later. You can expand your discussion about the verb *walk* by asking when (early, late) and how (quickly, slowly).

CLARIFYING CONJUNCTIONS, PRONOUNS, AND INTERJECTIONS

The lesson presentation continues: "Sometimes speakers and writers want to combine words, phrases, or clauses, so they need another part of speech to do that—a conjunction. A conjunction joins words, phrases, and clauses." (Remember to include a simple definition of each of the parts of speech as you introduce the concept of "parts of speech.")

Going on: "When speaking or writing, we sound repetitive or boring if we keep saying the same noun over and over again to refer to the same person, place, thing, activity, or event. So we sometimes replace a noun with a pronoun. A pronoun replaces or stands for a noun. Pronouns change forms to indicate whether the noun being replaced is masculine, feminine, or neither, and to indicate whether we're talking about one noun or several."

By this time, as you have been adding the names of the part of speech to the balloon drawing, most of the students are getting the picture and can offer correct examples of the different forms of pronouns. This shows that though they may not know the rules of grammar, many of them know how the language works grammatically! Some of your English language learners may perk up and comment that in their language, the forms of pronouns change in much the same way. This is good, because the next part of speech—the preposition—often throws them a curve.

Continue with the lesson: "Sometimes speakers and writers want to show the relationship between a noun or pronoun and some other word in a sentence. They want to indicate the place or position of the other noun or pronoun. To communicate this, they use yet another part of speech—the preposition. A preposition shows the relationship between a noun or pronoun and another word in the sentence.

"Look at this marker I'm using. Suppose I want to communicate to others that the marker is *in* my hand or *on* my desk, or *under* the table. Notice that some of these words show the relationship or place of the noun—'the marker'—in relation to my hand, the desk, or the table. Those words are prepositions (notice the root *position*). Suppose I put the marker here (hold the marker above the head)? What word tells the position or relationship of the marker to my head (*above* or *over*)? What word shows this relationship or position (*behind*)?" By now, students usually understand the concept or function of the preposition.

Next, deal with the interjection. "This last common part of speech does not name, show action, modify or limit, join, replace, or show relationship or position. But because it serves an entirely different function in communicating; it is another part of speech. This eighth part of speech identifies those words that interrupt a flow of thought to express mild or strong emotions. This part of speech is called an interjection."

An *interjection* exclaims emotions and has no other grammatical connection in the sentence. The word *interjection* comes from a Latin prefix *inter*, which means *between* and a root word *ject* that means "to throw" (as in "project" to throw forward or "reject" to throw back). Speakers and writers sometimes "throw" in words to show emotion, like *wow, darn, ouch,* or *hey*! For this eighth part of speech, invite students to suggest those words that speakers and writers throw into their communication between other ideas as interjections. Be prepared for them to get silly and try to throw in "no-no" words.

PULLING THE PARTS TOGETHER

Finally, a classroom dénouement: by this time, you have completed the drawing with names of the eight parts of speech all within the balloon, graphically illustrating that speech is made of different parts, each serving a specific purpose to communicate clearly exactly what we want to get across to our listeners or readers. And so, you conclude the following:

"These, ladies and gentlemen, are the eight common parts of speech. Each has a different function in communicating what we speak or write. The more precisely you use parts of speech, the more likely the ideas you have are transferred clearly and accurately to your listeners and readers.

"As you continue studying grammar, you'll learn ways that parts of speech are used in different ways in sentences. You soon learn that groups of words—phrases and clauses—can function as a unit the same way that single-word parts of speech function.

"The key for you to remember is the part that each of these single words or single units of words plays in communicating ideas. As you learn these functions and put them into practice in your own speaking and writing, each of you can become a better speaker and writer, getting across to the listener/reader more exactly the ideas you want to communicate."

Introducing or reviewing the parts of speech according to their function in the sentence prepares for an easy transition to teaching phrases, verbals, and clauses. When students see a prepositional phrase that modifies a noun—answering the same kinds of questions that single-word adjectives answer—they can understand adjective phrases. For example, "Please bring me the box *in the closet*, not the one *under my bed*." Or when the students see a sentence in which a prepositional phrase answers questions about verbs in the same way that single-word adverbs do, the students get the idea of adverb phrases. For example, "Ahmad reached *into his pocket* to get his cell phone."

The same transfer of conceptual understanding seems to flow when students encounter verbals; those that name actions (gerunds), "*Walking* is good exercise, so my grandfather gets up early and walks three blocks just to get his first cup of coffee." Similarly, they can understand when they see verbs describing nouns (participles). "My grandmother still has the *carving* knife her mother received as a wedding gift." You get the point. Taking the time to teach parts of speech as functions of communication makes it easier for students to see the patterns in the language, even in more sophisticated settings.

ILLUSTRATING WHY SYNTAX MATTERS

In the middle grades, the curriculum usually moves beyond parts of both speech and sentences to phrases, verbals, clauses, and confusion-causing dangling modifiers. One of the ways to help students understand how much they use syntax (the order of words) to make sense of what they hear and read is to have them draw what they hear or see. To illustrate the concept of dangling modifiers, ask students to draw as precisely as possible sentences that you verbalize or project one at a time. Or, if using printout, you could ask half the students to draw the even numbered sentences and the other half to draw the odd numbered sentences. This way they read them all, draw half, and then see examples of the ones you find or those that follow:

1. A group of students was watching the show in their cars.
2. The track star twisted his ankle with the green sweatshirt.
3. I learned about the cat that was lost on the Internet.
4. Punctured by a nail, I had to repair my bike tire.
5. Reading e-mail on my cell phone, my cat crawled into my lap.

6. Locked in the trunk, my sister found my diary.
7. Our class gave gift bags to all the children filled with raisins.
8. Growing in the garden, I picked a bushel of green beans.
9. We saw a mountain lion hiking along with our binoculars.
10. I noticed an accident turning the corner.

You are right—doing these drawings evokes snorts and sniggles. That is just fine. Your students reflect on their own work and fear this may be the response others have to their speaking and writing. Thankfully, the activity illustrates emphatically that sentence syntax does influence communication. Afterward, your students become conscientious writers and work harder to avoid that confusion of imprecise language and sloppy grammar.

PATTERNING WITH PURPOSE: TEACH SYNTAX AND SENTENCE VARIETY

Another way to make grammar come alive for students is to examine sentence patterns in the writing of published authors—fiction and nonfiction. Sometimes, to demonstrate to students that they can write similarly powerful sentence styles and grammatical patterns, ask them to model a piece of their own prose after a short passage from the literature they are studying. You could select specific sentences yourself and have all the students pattern the same sentences. Better yet, ask students to locate in a recent reading assignment two or three sentences they find interesting.

Next, ask them to pattern their chosen sentences on a topic of their choice and then tell what makes the sentences appealing and if patterning them is a challenge. This kind of practice is particularly effective for English language learners and for students who may not hear Standard English spoken much at home. Patterning is a way to train the eyes and ears to speak and write fluently.

Think about the evocative paragraphs students could write based on the Elie Wiesel's memoir, *Night*. Consider using the "Never shall I forget"[2]passage, which describes Wiesel's first night in the concentration camp. Similar remarkable writing occurs when students pattern the distinctive sentence structures from literary works by classical writers like Hemingway, Twain, and Fitzgerald and contemporary ones like those you currently are teaching. Paying close attention to the way published writers organize their sentences helps students understand the power of word order and word choice.

Middle school students and English language learners often have sophisticated ideas but cannot easily write comparably complex grammatical structures to convey these thoughts. You can help them express themselves more fully and more adeptly. One helpful book is Harry R. Noden's *Image Grammar: Using Grammatical Structures to Teach Writing*. Noden offers students a variety of sentence starts, modifying strategies, and sentence endings to pattern. Doing activities from *Image Grammar*, your students can practice varying their structure and creating more interesting sentences as they write fiction and nonfiction in English and other classes across the content areas. A number of online resources provide comparable lessons you can adapt to fit the range of interests and needs of your learners.

PATTERNING CAN JUMP START ENGLISH LANGUAGE LEARNERS

You likely have heard the admonition to students editing their papers to "Just read it aloud." That works in some cases, but your ELL students may not have developed "an ear" to recognize Standard English even if they are intellectually sharp with fascinating ideas to share. Reading their writings aloud may not be enough to give students with an untrained ear the helpful clues they need for revision.

You can help them jump start their English composition and avoid feeling hampered even by simple English language vocabulary or sentence structures they have already learned. How? By encouraging them to pattern sentences. They become more comfortable writing on their own if they are following the syntax of writing passages that you recommend. For some reason, paying close attention to the way that published authors structure sentences can speed the process and increase the confidence limited English speakers have in writing freely.

Another idea for ear training comes from Dr. Arlene Mulligan who used drama to help her new English speakers improve their sentence syntax. She writes,

"Because second language learners, by necessity, must be acute listeners, they already have developed . . . ears sensitive to differences in diction, dialect, and speech patterns. Most of these young people are very bright and are attentive to the spoken word."[3]

Mulligan invites her new English speakers to write drama and to incorporate considerable dialogue in their writing. This invitation inspires these writers to attune their ears to the rhythms of spoken English and to imitate these patterns in their writing.

TEACHING GRAMMAR WITH RECORDED BOOKS

The oral language students hear in informal situations is not likely to be entirely Standard English. By encouraging them to attentively pattern the spoken word, we can help them train their ears for linguistic rhythms. This would be another reason to use audiobooks in your teaching. The more often all your students tune in to the rhythm and syntax of spoken English, the sooner they are likely to imitate it in their own speaking and writing. Conduct some research on your own to locate and create lists of appropriate audiobooks. Then you can recommend that your learners across the board listen regularly to good readers of recorded books on the Internet, or downloaded onto student iPods or cell phones.

HONORING HOME AND HEART LANGUAGES

In a culturally sustainable classroom, teachers are careful to avoid disparaging a student's home language or dialect; instead, they honor it. It's the way students communicate with those they love, respect, and care about. It's their heart and heritage language. To show that honor, these same sensitive teachers design lessons for which students are encouraged to incorporate this heart language into their writing and speaking. Some assignments may be creative writing for which students are asked to write realistic dialogue, keeping in mind their audience is their teacher and classmates. Spoken word assignments are another way in which students use words, phrases, and dialects that reflect the stories they're telling, the tone they wish to portray, and the mood they wish to elicit.

GRADING FOR GRAMMAR—NOT ALWAYS

After teaching a new concept, you could give a short writing assignment to see how well the students can apply it. The National Writing Project calls this "primary trait" grading. An alternative way to have students practice a newly taught or reviewed concept is to assign journal entries. At the beginning of the class period while you take attendance or collect homework, you could have students write a few sentences about a piece of literature they are studying. The twist, in this situation, is that you could require them to write using the newly taught grammar or syntax concept, such as using only active voice, or using three different kinds of sentences, or beginning each sentence with a different grammatical structure.

These five- or ten- minute writing assignments allow students to practice, demonstrate the forms one can use to communicate clearly, and produce for discussion examples of problems that can arise when writers do not follow the rules. These kinds of writings should not be collected or graded. Instead, simply have the students exchange journals, read them, and comment to their partner about what meets the assignment and what does not. Encourage

Plan class days for speaking only Standard English

students to discuss what changes need to be made to make the sentences correct in this setting. Then move on to the lesson of the day. Easy. Quick. Writing. Reading. Talking. Reviewing. Reinforcing.

ANALYZING THE GRAMMAR OF MEDIA

For decades, English language arts educators have taught students the grammar rules for writing and the grammar rules of literature (plot structure for fiction, text structure for nonfiction, and more recently peritext for web pages), but only few have had the confidence to teach the grammar of media. Twenty-first-century students view other print and electronic media many more hours per day than they view/read traditional books. For this reason, you are beginning to see media literacy among the standards to which you are to teach. The anchor standards require curricula to include assessment to determine how well students can "Integrate and evaluate information presented in diverse media and formats, including visually, quantitatively, and orally."[4] You can design lessons to teach your students how to "read the media" found in magazines and film, as well as on websites.

Lots of resources are on the Internet on such sites as Edutopia.org, which include interviews about the value of teaching the grammar of media literacy and a variety of video clips to use for classroom instruction. Or you can just use magazines you collect and keep in your classroom, or digital files of images you compile and project in programs like PowerPoint or Prezi.

Some simple lessons introduce the students to the use of color and layout. Other more in-depth lessons may involve learning the language of film—camera angles, use of lighting, timing of shots, and numbers of cuts—viewing samples, and then in groups, students creating short video or web pages that illustrate the concepts you are teaching.

DECONSTRUCTING THE GRAMMAR OF MEDIA

Check out a collection of lesson plans developed by the Center for Media Literacy (CML), which includes Five Key Questions and Five Core Concepts.[5]

Five Key Questions:

1. Who created this message?
2. What creative techniques are used to attract my attention?
3. How might different people understand this message differently?
4. What values, lifestyles, and points of view are represented in, or omitted from, this message?
5. Why is this message being sent?

Five Core Concepts:

1. All media messages are constructed.
2. Media messages are constructed using a creative language with its own rules.
3. Different people experience the same media message differently.
4. Media have embedded values and points of view.
5. Most media messages are organized to gain profit and power.

You can give these same students assignments to practice communicating in these media, too. Instead of requiring each unit of study to include only writing to show what students know, offer options for them to represent graphically what they are learning. Assign PowerPoint, Prezi, or Google slide presentations, cartooning, photography, and video as ways to show what they understand about the literature they read and the life they live and observe. With your students, create rubrics that refer to elements of layout, color, and design that you teach about the media they view. Becoming critical viewers is just the first step in understanding the grammar of the media. Producing that media is the step that shows that learning is taking place.

Colors and Colors

Even if your students reflect relatively homogenous cultural, racial, and ethnic backgrounds, they likely have different ideas about what colors mean. This difference will occur even more often when you have a diverse student population and read literature written by and for people from different countries and cultures. So it can be useful to include lessons that show the positive and negative connotations of colors as well as what they signify in different countries. This can deepen students' insight into literature when they attune themselves to intentional use of color in the texts they read and view.

For example, the color white in Western countries means innocence and purity and often is worn by brides; in India, white is the color of mourning, and widows wear white. Red in some countries connotes anger, rage, and danger; but in some countries like India, red is worn by Hindu brides to represent prosperity and fertility. Blue has both positive and negative connotations just in the United States! And we're not talking about the colors of college rivals! Blue could stand for sadness and sorrow; it also could stand for loyalty and patriotism if one is described as "true blue!"

Assessing News Grammar and Connecting to Literature

This news-related assignment requires students to conduct research, practice citation and documentation, and think more critically about persuasive techniques. During the first two weeks of this month-long assignment, they are to select a topic reported in a print or digital medium, then bring in copies of four or five written articles on the same topic. They can also use text transcriptions of television reports available on local and network websites. If your students have access to the Internet, they can follow the news easily. The purpose is to have them watch the news for a month and be prepared to assess ways the nonfiction writing is the same or different than the text structure of fiction studied in class. How does it work?

After students have read opening chapters, are through the exposition of the fictional text, and have a solid sense of the personalities of the characters, you could ask students to write a brief rationale explaining why a chosen literary character would be interested in some current events and what would be that character's response to those particular news stories. For example:

- Why would Jem in *To Kill a Mockingbird* be interested in a trial reported in news media? What would he say about the verdict?
- Why would Mercutio or Benvolio in *Romeo and Juliet* be interested in curfew laws that require teenagers to be at home before 10 p.m.? What arguments for and against them?

- Why would Panchito from *The Circuit* or Esperanza from *Esperanza Rising* be interested in educational opportunities for undocumented immigrants? How would these characters advocate for more?

As you and the class continue studying the novel, the students can be gathering information to flesh out their persuasive speeches. See chapter 4 for persuasive writing strategies, which can be applied to persuasive speech writing, and chapter 7 for delivery of persuasive presentations.

Consider cross-curricular assignments for which students can write a speech in your class based on a topic they are studying in history, science, music, or math. Depending on your school setting and the access your students have to resources, you may need to allot in-class time for research, as well as for practicing the speeches once they are written.

This kind of multigenre and interdisciplinary assignment, looking at fiction and nonfiction concurrently in both print and electronic media, helps students make text-world connections. They see that times change but people don't—a universal quality of good literature.

Since a portion of the assignment requires students to justify their reasons for choosing specific news articles and relating them to fictional characters, this assignment requires your readers to consider the ways fiction authors reveal the personalities and motivations of characters in the stories students already have studied. Finally, incorporating a speech based on real news articles in the same instructional unit as the study of a novel gives students a chance to detect the different text structures used in fiction and nonfiction, a critical-thinking skill most schools expect their students to acquire.

Shoring Up Shy Students

Consider these ideas for shy students who want to be "right" before they speak up in class as you have them practicing Standard English in class discussion and to talk about media.

- *Think-pair-share* during which students write their response, pair with a partner to compare/revise answers, and then share with whole class.
- *Sentence Starters*—Your students may not yet be comfortable with the "language" of literary analysis. See online resources for sentence starters and stems for talking about reading, writing, and viewing.
- *Project* or *post literary terms*, *text structures*, and *media terms* where students can see them during discussions about literature, writing, or media. These visual prompts will encourage them to consider the traits and use the terminology.

- *Sketch to Stretch*—Some students think better with pencil in hand as they doodle, diagram, or draw. Invite those who wish to sketch their thoughts to do that. Then, if phone cameras are available, have them photograph their drawing and send it to you to project for the class to view. Sharing such responses will invite comments from those still a little shy about sharing words, expand ideas about the texts, and provide no-stress assessment for you, giving insight into what even your shyest students are thinking and grasping about what you're teaching.
- *Use colors.* Invite students to use significance of color. For example, if you were to use colors to show the personality of the characters in this story, what would they be and why? What colors suggest the tone and mood of this story (your story)? Good time to review that *T*one is au*T*hor's a*TT*itude *t*oward *T*opic, while *M*ood answers "How does this text *M*ake '*Me*' the reader feel"? (When teaching this concept, show the T for tone, author, attitude, and topic with T in big letters or different colors, and show link between Mood and Me. The visual learners remember that graphic depiction.) See the companion website for this book for resources to review cultures and colors.

DAY	RED	GREEN	PURPLE	ORANGE	BLUE
1	SPEAKING (NO FEEDBACK)	Comment on *CONTENT* (Appropriate for audience, variety of support, appeals, quality of evidence and resources, sources cited, etc.)	Comment on *ORGANIZATION* (Introduction with SIGN POST (statement of purpose)) TRANSITIONS (appropriate for kind of speech) CONCLUSION (summary, reflection, or projection without introducing new ideas)	Comment on *VOCAL ISSUES* (Articulation, intonation, pace, pauses, volume, etc.)	Comment on *APPEARANCE* (Appropriate gestures, use of physical space, visual aids, etc.)
2	APPEARANCE	SPEAKING	CONTENT	ORGANIZATION	VOCAL ISSUES
3	VOCAL ISSUES	APPEARANCE	SPEAKING	CONTENT	ORGANIZATION
4	ORGANIZATION	VOCAL ISSUES	APPEARANCE	SPEAKING	CONTENT
5	CONTENT	ORGANIZATION	VOCAL ISSUES	APPEARANCE	SPEAKING

Chart to schedule a week of speeches with assignments for feedback

CONCLUSION

When students have personal reasons for code-switching or code-blending to communicate in the grammar of Standard English, they usually are amenable to learning how to do so. Whether writing for a specific purpose to a real audience, presenting a speech in class, or talking with peers, students want to be seen as smart enough to use appropriate language. You can help them expand their knowledge and skills by incorporating regular opportunities to learn and use Standard English while honoring their home or heart languages.

Teaching students to view media with a critical eye helps them become defensive viewers and thoughtful creators in a variety of formats. They become more sensitive to the impact color, size, and design have on those with whom they wish to communicate.

Under your tutelage, students gain both the ability and self-assurance to travel with ease across this country and abroad, fairly certain they can adapt. As they mature and enter the world of work, they are less likely to be passed up for a job promotion because they will have the writing, representing, and speaking skills sought in twenty-first-century job markets.

NOTES

1. Clella Jaffe, "Introduction to Public Speaking and Culture." *Public Speaking: Concepts and Skills for a Diverse Society*, 5th ed., edited by Clella Jaffe. (Wadsworth/Thomas Learning: Belmont, CA, 2007), 6.
2. Elie Wiesel, *Night*. (New York: Bantam Books, 1960), 32.
3. Arlene Mulligan, 'Opening Doors' Drama with Second Language Learners." *Promising Practices: Unbearably Good Teacher-Tested Ideas*. (San Diego: The Greater San Diego Council of Teachers of English,1996), 72.
4. "English Language Arts Standards » Anchor Standards » College and Career Readiness Anchor Standards for Language," Common Core State Standards Initiative, 2011. http://www.corestandards.org/ELA-Literacy/CCRA/SL/2/ (accessed August 24 ,2018).
5. Fred Baker, "CML's Five Key Questions and Core Concepts of Media Literacy for Deconstruction," Media Lit, 2011. http://www.medialit.org/sites/default/files/14A_CCKQposter.pdf (accessed October 12, 2017).

Afterword

Bon Voyage:
Acknowledge the Challenge
and Maximize the Opportunity

Ideal teachers are those who use themselves as bridges over which they invite their students to cross, then having facilitated their crossing, joyfully collapse, encouraging them to create bridges of their own.[1]

—Nikos Kazantzakis

Be honest. Are you planning to teach where you are *because* or *until*? Over my years of experience across the nation, I have noticed that many new-to-middle school and new-to-community college teachers accept a position not because it is the fulfillment of a lifelong dream to teach preteenagers or adults starting college. They simply plan to settle in until an elementary or high school position opens, or they earn their PhD and start on the tenure track. Your reason really doesn't matter. If you conscientiously apply what you are learning in this book, you can be a successful educator wherever you are assigned.

Whether you are beginning your first, second, seventh, or seventeenth year of teaching, you are embarking on a trip of a lifetime. Each year of teaching can be different, unique, and surprisingly very much the same—an opportunity to learn and to inspire learning.

If you choose to remain at your current school, you will come to recognize that teaching young adolescents or adults starting their college careers in a community college can be pure joy. You soon realize that you are in the prime place, at a pivotal time in the lives of your students, a time when they either develop a healthy respect or a deep resentment for school. You discover the satisfaction in helping students discover how they learn while acquiring skills and consuming information.

Language arts is the one course students take nearly every year. Those who teach them well come to appreciate the time and flexibility to adjust

159

instruction in ways that enhance student learning across the curriculum and thus increase student enjoyment of schooling in general. Really?

The core components of the language arts curriculum—reading, writing, speaking, and listening—are skills that form the foundation for learning in all other academic courses. Proficiency in these areas is expected when these students enter their social studies, science, math classes, and more specialized courses in STEM. When such aptitude is missing or deficient, English teachers often are called on the carpet to explain why they are not doing their job. How should you respond? What can you do to reduce the angst when accused of being an ineffective educator?

First, acknowledge the challenge of teaching students of any age. Yes, most of them come to middle school in the throes of puberty, dealing with raging hormones; startling physical changes or lack thereof; distressing emotional roller coasters; and uncertainty about figuring out what all these different teachers want from them! Others begin community college doubtful of their ability to succeed.

For the first time, some middle school students have multiple teachers daily. There is not just one teacher who knows what Karilla likes and dislikes and how she learns best; one who makes allowances for Sydney when he's just moved from living with Dad for six months into the house with Mom, her current husband, and new baby; or one teacher who understands Juanita freezes when asked to read out loud without having time to practice. These students may have to learn their way around a larger school and even find a place to eat lunch with people they don't know. Community college students often have demanding families or are working full-time jobs. How can they attend to class work?

All this is just too much for some students. Add to it learning parts of speech and elements of fiction; how to research a contemporary topic; writing a persuasive essay on a controversial issue with correctly formatted endnotes, and then presenting the report out loud to the class with visual aids in a PowerPoint presentation! It is overwhelming to be expected to know which teachers will make Lailani work in small groups with Duong, the guy she has a crush on, and with Shakira, the girl she had a fight with during soccer practice. Anyway, Andrew's teacher last year didn't teach him how to use a Google Drive or Blackboard and all the rest of his classmates seem to know what the teacher's talking about. It's just too embarrassing; and why did Mom and Dad make Kwami come to this school anyway! Why did I think that I, an adult who's been out of school for years, can succeed now?

At the same time, language arts teachers have a curriculum to cover, a set of English language arts standards that each student must reach, and parents who expect teachers to do what they may not be able to do—keep Sally and Salvador happy. How can teachers of young adolescents and new college students be professionally effective and personally satisfied enough to feel successful in this setting?

Maximize the opportunity. Students want to learn, and they thrive with educators willing to learn how to teach such willing students—as individuals, not as receptacles of information. Research in the past thirty years has revealed what experienced teachers have suspected: their classes reflect multiple intelligences and students who learn in different ways; culture makes a difference; and males learn better in certain settings than females do. The researchers urge teachers to adapt instruction to enhance all learning. No, this does not mean creating individualized educational plans for every student you teach. It does mean designing lessons that teach the same lesson in a variety of ways and offer students choices in how they show what they know.

You are not alone on this journey even within your classroom. Your students are there to help. They may know the school, the community, and neighborhood better than you, so let them teach you the ropes—but keep in mind that you are a professional. You are the adult hired to see that all have safe passage through the sometimes tumultuous sea that is a year in the life of teenagers or new-to-college students. Keep your eyes on the goal and, using your peripheral vision, keep your students in view, too. They are who you are teaching. Yes, you are teaching human beings, not just content. With patience and persistence, you all can reach the shore safely, secure in the knowledge you have gained and the skills you have honed. You, their guide, can be assured that you can reach the shore intact by

- carefully planning lessons based on what you know about the curriculum and what you learn about your students each school year;
- observing and documenting what goes on in your classes;
- varying the kind of performance and product assessments you assign;
- being willing to modify your lessons to meet the needs and interests of your students;
- being firm but fair in your interactions with students, colleagues, parents, and guardians;
- borrowing freely and sharing generously with colleagues across the content areas;
- recognizing that help is available—right in this book, right in your classroom, and from your students, your fellow travelers on this journey;
- taking time each week to refresh yourself, spending time with family and friends, or reading a good book;
- attending, every year, at least one conference, seminar, or workshop for professional and personal enrichment; and
- believing that associating with excited, enthusiastic, and experienced educators is the best way to maintain your passion for the profession.

Careful planning leads to smoother sailing

Know that as you teach your students to understand and use language arts to receive information and express themselves, you are giving them the golden tickets to academic success, career enrichment, and personal satisfaction. You, their language arts teacher, have the privilege of guiding and coaching these students along the journey. You, who provide the balance between dependable discipline and appropriate play in a safe, supportive, culturally sustaining environment, can help raise their self-esteem and increase their confidence and competence in communicating.

What does this look like in the real world? For some classes, it means incorporating more variety in your teaching. It means recognizing that students come to you with access to a range of technology; it is your job to help them understand educational applications and encourage them to use what they know to learn what you teach. This will prepare them for careers or colleges, wherever the next leg of their journey takes them.

So, whether you are teaching in middle school, high school, or community college—because it is your dream job or until you get an assignment teaching a different grade or at a four-year college—you have recognized the challenge and are maximizing the opportunity to teach and enjoy each student as a unique individual. Do what you can to make these crucial years for your students ones during which they learn to love learning.

Each time you design flexible lessons permeated with rich experiences for exploring fiction and nonfiction in the print and electronic media; of writing in a range of modes for a variety of authentic purposes; by talking and listening to you, their peers, and those they encounter face-to-face and online while learning to critically view and use technology, you are cultivating vital skills for growth. With diligence on your part and assiduousness on theirs, you all will complete a school year inspired by the success of the current year, eager to move on to the challenges of the next.

So, bon voyage! Enjoy the journey!

NOTE

1. Nikos Kazantzakis, "Quotes by Nikos Kazantzakis," Goodreads, 2011. http://www.goodreads.com/quotes/show/301968 (accessed April 5, 2012).

Bibliography

"Adolescent Brain Development." ACT for Youth Upstate Center of Excellence. A collaboration of Cornell University, University of Rochester, and the NYS Center for School Safety Upstate Center of Excellence, May 2012. http://www. actforyouth.net/resources/rf/rf_brain_0502.pdf (accessed April 6, 2012).

Bacon, Francis. "Essays of Francis Bacon—Of Studies." Authorama Public Domain Books, n.d. http://www.authorama.com/essays-of-francis-bacon-50.html (accessed March 8, 2012).

Baker, Fred. "CML's Five Key Questions and Core Concepts of Media Literacy for Deconstruction." Center for Media Literacy, 2011. http://www.medialit.org/sites/ default/files/14A_CCKQposter.pdf (accessed June 14, 2012).

Hendrix, Sybylla Y. "Why Our Students Study Literature." Gustavus Adolphus College, n.d. http://gustavus.edu/academics/english/whystudyliterature.php (accessed April 3, 2012).

"English Language Arts Standards » Anchor Standards » College and Career Readiness Anchor Standards for Reading." English Language Arts Standards » Reading: Informational Text » Grade 8 | Common Core State Standards Initiative. http:// www.corestandards.org/ELA-Literacy/CCRA/R/#CCSS.ELA-Literacy.CCRA.R.8 (accessed September 22, 2018).

Epstein, Joseph. "The Personal Essay: A Form of Discovery." In *The Norton Book of Personal Essays*, edited by Joseph Epstein. New York: Norton, 1997.

Estrada, Ignacio "Nacho." Think Exist, n.d. http://thinkexist.com/quotes/ignacio_ estrada/ (accessed May 31, 2012).

Franklin, Benjamin. Finest Quotes, n.d. http://izquotes.com/quote/283028 (accessed January 2, 2018).

Genevieve, Nancy. "Finalists." In *American Religion and Literature Society Newsletter*, edited by Deshae Lott. Savannah, GA: Department of Liberal Arts, Savannah State University. (Spring 2007).

———. *NYX: Daughter of Chaos*. Eureka: NOX Press, 2002.

————. *NYX: Mother of Light*. Eureka: NOX Press, 2001 and ELM 5, no. 2 (Spring 1997).

Hanson, Heather. "Speak English Clearly and Grammatically, and Boost Your Success!" Articles Base, n.d. http://leadershiptrainingtutorials.com/leadership-training/uncategorized/speak-english-clearly-and-grammatically-and-boost-your-success/#.W4AnyOhKhAE (accessed August 24, 2018).

Houghton Mifflin College Dictionary. Boston: Houghton Mifflin, 1986.

Jaffe, Clella. "Introduction to Public Speaking and Culture." In *Public Speaking: Concepts and Skills for a Diverse Society*, 5th ed., edited by Clella Jaffe. Boston: Wadsworth, 2007.

Kazantzakis Nikos, "Quotes by Nikos Kazantzakis," Goodreads, 2011. http://www.goodreads.com/quotes/show/301968 (accessed April 5, 2012).

Mulligan, Arlene. "Opening Doors: Drama with Second Language Learners." In *Promising Practices: Unbearably Good, Teacher Tested Ideas*, edited by Linda Scott. San Diego: Greater San Diego Council of Teachers of English, 1996.

Oliver, Mary. *New and Selected Poems: Volume One*. Boston, MA: Beacon Press, 1992.

Pascal, Blaise. Brainy Quotes, 2009. https://www.brainyquote.com/quotes/blaise_pascal_133403 (accessed January 2, 2018).

Reutzel, D. Ray and Robert B. Cooter. *Strategies for Reading Assessment and Instruction: Helping Every Child Succeed*. Upper Saddle River, NJ: Merrill Prentice Hall, 2003.

Roseboro, Anna J. Small. "Professional and Personal Lives." *California English* 16, no.1 (September 2010): 8–9.

Troupe, Quincy. "My Poems Have Holes Sewn into Them." In *Transcircularities: New and Selected Poems*, edited by Quincy Troupe, 98–99. Minneapolis: Coffee House Press, 2002.

Ward, William Arthur. "Quotes about Teaching," National Education Association, 2012. https://www.brainyquote.com/quotes/william_arthur_ward_103463 (accessed August 24, 2018).

Wiesel, Elie. *Night*. New York: Bantam, 1982.

Extended Acknowledgments

Thanks to these educators who field-tested various strategies, wrote up, and sent me their reflections. See their full write-ups on my website at www. teachingenglishlanguagearts.com

Cresence Birder

English teacher of ninth-grade students at The Bishop's School, La Jolla, California, Independent School.

Anne Brown

English teacher of sixth-to-eighth-grade students at the Crestwood Middle School, Kentwood, Michigan.

José Luis Cano

Adjunct instructor of adult students at the Texas Southernmost College, Brownsville, Texas.

Kiondre Dunnam

Social studies teacher of seventh-grade students at the W. R. Coile Middle School, Athens, Georgia.

Cassidy Earle (Greer)

Teacher for sixth-grade math students at the Hopewell Middle School, Milton, Georgia.

Emily Espy

Teacher of eighth-grade math students at Dorchester Charter School in Boston, Massachusetts.

Kalpana Iyengar

PhD, lecturer to preservice teachers, University of Texas in San Antonio, Texas.

Claudia A. Marschall

Retired English and drama teacher at Buffalo Academy for Visual and Performing Arts High School, Buffalo, New York. Current mentor to Early Career ELA teachers through National Council of Teachers of English.

Jazmen Moore

Teacher of English literature to sophomores and interdisciplinary world studies class to freshman at Oak Park and River Forest High School in Oak Park, Illinois.

Ellen Murray, M.Ed.

Retired reading specialist and current consultant and designer of Think, Spell, Write, Reading Program in Kent County, Michigan.

Howard Smith

Associate professor of Bicultural and Bilingual Studies for Preservice Teachers in College of Education and Human Development at University of Texas in San Antonio, Texas.

Audrey Spica

Teacher of English to seventh-grade students at the Pinewood Middle School in Kentwood, Michigan.

About the Author

Anna J. Small Roseboro, a National Board Certified Teacher, has over four decades experience teaching in public and private schools, mentoring early career educators, and facilitating leadership institutes. She was awarded Distinguished Service Awards by the California Association of Teachers of English (2009) and the National Council of Teachers of English (2016).

Mrs. Roseboro earned a BA in speech communications from Wayne State University and an MA in curriculum design from the University of California, San Diego. Her research investigated the link between writing to learn and retention in mathematics. She earned the Early Adolescent/English Language Arts Certificate from the National Board of Professional Teaching Standards in 1998.

Mrs. Roseboro represented Rotary International in a group-study exchange with educators in East Africa. In addition to teaching young adolescents in Michigan, Missouri, New York, Massachusetts, and California, she has taught adults at the Rochester Theological Institute, Grand Valley State University, and Calvin College. She served sixteen years as director of summer session programs for students in grades five through twelve, coached a National Forensic League competitive speech team for twelve years, and was English Department chair from 1999 to 2005 at the Bishop's School. In 2008–2009, Anna was a faculty leader at the NCTE Affiliate and Leadership Conference and served as master teacher for the San Francisco Bay Area Teachers Center in an online teaching environment.

Her articles have appeared in the *English Journal, English Leadership Quarterly, Fine Lines*—a national quarterly creative writing journal, and *California English*. She has published three texts for teachers: *Teaching Middle School Language Arts* (2010), *Teaching Writing in the Middle School* (2013), and *Teaching Reading in the Middle School* (2013); a novel and a poetry book for young people. Her writing appears in online professional blogs, in online communities for teachers such as English Companion and the Teaching and Learning Forum, and in *Continuing the Journey: Becoming a Better Teacher of Literature and Informational Texts* (2017).

Since her retirement, Mrs. Roseboro serves as codirector of the Conference on English Education Commission to Support Early Career English Language Arts Teachers and of the National Council of Teachers of English Early Career Educators of Color Leadership Award Program.